ALLEN RIDER GUIDES

RIDING IN A POINT-TO-POINT

ALLEN RIDER GUIDES

Riding in a Point-to-Point
Anne Holland

J. A. Allen

London

British Library Cataloguing in Publication Data

Holland, Anne
Riding in a Point-to-point. − (Allen Rider
Guide Series)
I. Title II. Series
798.4

ISBN 0−85131−554−2

Published in Great Britain by
J. A. Allen & Company Limited,
1, Lower Grosvenor Place, Buckingham Palace Road, London, SW1W OEL

© J. A. Allen & Co., 1992

Text illustrations Maggie Raynor
Text and cover design Nancy Lawrence

Printed in Hong Kong by Dah Hua Printing Co. Ltd.,
Typeset in Hong Kong by Setrite Typesetters Ltd.

Contents

— Contents —

Editor's note

Point-to-pointing is a sport with a strong sense of tradition and, in common with British National Hunt racing, all measurements of weight and distance are made, and given, in imperial units only. For this reason, where such measurements are mentioned in this text, the imperial system is adhered to. Readers unfamiliar with the imperial system may find the following of assistance:

The standard length of a point-to-point race is 3 miles, which represents 4.83 km. However, some races are now run over 2½ miles (4.03 km.), and a few are over 4 miles (6.44 km.).

The total range of weights carried by horses in point-to-point varies from 10 st. 7 lb. to 13 st. (66.80 kg. to 82.72 kg.). The imperial pound (lb.) is equivalent to .454 kg. and the imperial stone is equivalent to 6.36 kg., or 14 lb.

Acknowledgements

My thanks go to all those who helped in the preparation of this book. I am indebted to Simon Claisse, Jockey Club Controller of Point-to-Points, for checking and correcting information, making constructive suggestions, and bringing the rules totally up to date; to David Tatlow, four times champion rider, for his expert advice on race-riding; and to Jane Nixon, M.R.C.V.S.

My thanks also go to Caroline Burt of J.A. Allen & Co; Hugh Condry of *Horse and Hound*; Sarah Dawson; Edwyn Good, clerk of the course, Kimble; Amanda Hamilton-Fairley; Caroline Saunders; Vera Steggles and all others who have given help and encouragement.

Anne Holland

List of Illustrations

Introduction

Picnics, wellies, Barbours, binoculars, booze, all the para-phernalia for a day at the local point-to-point is packed into the car boot, a duster hoisted on to the car aerial as a landmark for the children. In the distance the bookies are calling the odds for the first race and soon the horses are galloping past, hooves thundering, streaming over the fences, their jockeys bright in their distinctive colours, an inspiration to many youngsters.

It was in 1752 that one Edmund Blake bet a certain Cornelius O'Callaghan a cask of wine that his hunter could beat the other's racing from Buttevant church spire to the steeple of St. Leger, Doneraile, nearly five miles distant over Co Cork countryside.

News of the challenge soon spread; flat racing had existed for years but this was something quite different − there were going to be *obstacles* in the way!

Excitement reached fever pitch as people flocked from miles around to witness the novel spectacle. Over blind banks and ditches the contestants ran, the steeple of the church built by Sir William St. Leger sometimes hidden by the hills. On they galloped, each determined to prove his hunter the superior, falling into ditches, crashing through thorn-topped banks, flying the occasional stone wall, crossing 'bohereens' or narrow tracks.

Alas, history does not relate who actually won the race, but the pair deserve their place equally in history for having started racing across country from point to point, chasing distant steeples. It was the start of a tradition that, above all, produces real sportsmanship.

Rules for point-to-pointing were first introduced by the National Hunt Committee in the 1880s when to their consternation the amateur sport seemed to be gaining more popularity than professional steeplechasing. In 1882 they decreed that point-to-points need not be advertised and that horses running in them should not be disqualified from running in races under National Hunt (N.H.) rules. They also said no point-to-point course should be defined, in contrast to steeplechasing which had begun to have man-made fences in about 1810; furthermore, while racing colours had been introduced to steeplechasing in 1804, hunting dress continued to be worn in point-to-points until around the beginning of the Second World War.

In 1889, the N.H. Committee decreed that each hunt could have only one point-to-point meeting per year, and no course could be used for more than one meeting, except by special permission. Admission charges were banned (as they are still, gate money coming from car entrance not individuals). No race could be over less than three miles, and this held until 1990 when, as an experiment, certain maiden races were allowed to be run over two and a half miles; and no prize greater than £20 could be awarded. This sum did not change until 1961.

About the turn of the century point-to-point courses were marked out by flags but, as late as 1935, the Equitation School at Weedon still refused to divulge in advance where the course was to run.

It was when birch fences on defined point-to-point courses came into being in the 1920s that point-to-pointing really became amateur steeplechasing, although an attempt has been made in recent years to revive the old fashioned point-to-point with cross-country members races being allowed in addition to the rest of the card. In 1982, there were ten such races, sponsored by Buchanan, with fields averaging twenty runners; thirteen races in 1983 drew a similar average. In 1991 only six hunts staged such a race, the Puckeridge and Thurlow in East Anglia, the Lauderdale in Scotland, the Old Surrey and Burstow, the High Peak and North East Cheshire Drag, the Cottesmore in Leicestershire and the Cattistock in Dorset. The Beaufort's race, which drew thirty-nine runners in 1982, fielded only twelve in 1989 after which the hunt ceased to stage it. Similarly the Worcestershire, which had twenty runners in the first year, had only three in 1989, and then also stopped. The six races held in 1990 drew a total of seventy runners. Any hunt may apply for such a race provided it can provide a suitable course, and promoting hunts find them good for attracting local sponsors as they attract a local crowd supporting friends 'having a go' on their genuine hunters. Perhaps the way to reverse the decline would be to allow runners from other local hunts to compete.

It was in the 1920s, much to male riders' surprise, that men suddenly found women racing against them, the N.H. Committee rules governing the sport having not specifically banned them; and to find women not only riding against them but also beating them was more than they could bear. So ladies races were introduced, and between 1930 and 1967 women were not allowed to contest any other races. As the vast majority of these races were adjacent hunts ladies races, they were able to contest only a handful of races per year.

At last, in 1967, they were allowed to ride against the men in hunt members races, but only if the promoting point-to-point committee decided to include this in their conditions. In 1976 all races with the exception of men's opens were opened up to lady riders, in spite of considerable protest that women should not be allowed to ride in maiden races because of the higher risk. The only exception to women riding in open races was on a card where no ladies open was included, which results in one 'mixed' open; of the few such mixed opens staged probably the best known are those at Tweseldown and for the Coronation Cup at Larkhill.

It was only after the Second World War that ex-racehorses began to infiltrate the point-to-point ranks, but it was the First World War that sounded the death knell of 'old-fashioned' point-to-pointing when not only were so many of the country's 'young bloods' killed in service but so were thousands of the very horses they would have been competing on 'between the flags'.

Almost all point-to-points are run by hunts, for whom they provide a good social day out as well as a fund raiser, and the hunting connection remains a strong link. All meetings are approved by the Jockey Club, including some meetings run by a club instead of a hunt, such as the Melton Hunt Club meeting in Leicestershire, which supports hunting with the Belvoir, Quorn and Cottesmore. The Pegasus Club Bar meeting at Little Horwood is run by the legal fraternity and dates back to 1895 (this meeting is not being run in 1992), and there is the Point-to-Point Owners Association meeting, a comparatively new venture, but again, run for the good of the sport.

The majority of the 200 meetings are held at venues that for the rest of the year revert to farmland, facilities being provided for the day by assorted tentage, the track being harrowed and rolled and roped off. A few meetings, however, have permanent buildings, a legacy from when they were once small N.H. courses; Tweseldown, for instance, Cottenham, Bogside, or the army buildings at Larkhill, while one or two courses run inside current N.H. tracks such as Fakenham, Wetherby and Aintree.

One of point-to-pointing's attractions lies in these many and diverse courses, often reflecting the locality: fences built between stone walls in Cornwall; the wooded, undulating East Sussex countryside at Heathfield where the gradients produce a number of drop fences and the bends produce opportunities for additional racecraft from the jockeys. Several hunts nowadays share a course, which helps reduce their running costs. Larkhill had six and Tweseldown seven fixtures each in 1991; Marks Tey in Essex (a course which features different length races) had three, while many will have two − but, for the majority it is still a once-a-year venue.

Today most of the tracks are prepared with good viewing in mind for the paying public and with regard to safety both of horses and humans. Point-to-pointing is a sport which combines tradition and atmosphere while at the same time moving with the times. It is also very much a family affair both for participants and spectators, and this gives it an advantage over many other sports. For those involved, the day at the races is the culmination of many months of hard work, while regular followers who have never owned or ridden a horse in their lives can feel involved as they get to know 'their' horses during the season.

The season is such a short one, from February to May, that many of the horses run week after week. There is no handicapping, so it is very often possible to follow a particular horse with considerable success, admittedly at short odds. Prize money is small and so no one is in it for the money. Those who over the years level the slur that point-to-pointing is too professional confuse the meaning of the word: although admittedly many livery proprietors are professional trainers and some owners may make money by selling a winner owners and riders will not be point-to-pointing for 'a livelihood or money' and there is nothing wrong with an amateur performing to a high standard; indeed, this is what should be aimed for.

1

So You Want to Point-to-Point?

The Spectrum of Riders

Today, point-to-point jockeys vary from the 'amateur amateur' who has a 'bump round' on his own horse and who is probably unfit as well as inexperienced, to those who ride out daily, have raced for years, and ridden many winners.

Many will come from backgrounds steeped in the sport, others will have been inspired by those family days out in the spring — all will be amateurs, those who 'cultivate a thing as a pastime', to quote the *Oxford Dictionary* definition. Nurses, accountants, builders, businessmen, farmers and those 'born on a horse' can and do ride alongside each other, many nurturing a recurring dream throughout their childhoods to ride in a point-to-point.

The Need for a Competitive Nature

Race-riding is a totally different form of equestrianism from any other, and much of it will be learnt through practice. Skill can be acquired beforehand by watching, riding out for a trainer, by listening and by getting oneself fit as well as the horse, but by far and away the most important aspect is to *want* to race. Only after that comes skill and ability. It's no good demanding that darling Dan does it because his grandfather was an ace rider, or in pushing prim Priscilla if her heart is not in it. However, if the idea of getting up at all hours to ride in the dark before going to work, going through months of tortuous wasting and exercising, travelling the length and breadth of Britain in search of a meeting that is not abandoned through frost or rain all in order to risk your neck for the sake of the odd paltry £100 prize does not appal you, then point-to-pointing is for you.

Only after this ambition to ride comes the question of ability but, even if all you want is a 'bump round in the members', the better it is done the greater will be the pleasure and reward. A corollary to this is that the competitive nature of the point-to-point rider will be such that you will not wish to go out with the idea of having no hope, even on a 'no-hoper'; you have got to believe that perhaps this is the day your horse will come good, or when all the others will fall down...

2

Buying a Point-to-Pointer

Some horses are expensively purchased and virtually professionally trained at livery, but many more are bargains picked up from public auction or, more rewarding still, bred by the owner, who is often the trainer and jockey as well.

Some 4,000 horses raced 'between the flags' in 1990. Many of them will never aspire to greater heights, while for others, the sport provides an ideal nursery for a young horse before going into N.H. racing and, what's more, an ideal retirement home for the older horse who has had his day on the racecourse proper.

Until 1990, all point-to-point races were run over a minimum of three miles, with just a few, mostly prestigious ones such as the Lord Grimthorpe Cup at the Middleton fixture, and the Lord Ashton of Hyde Cup at the Heythrop, run over longer distances.

As an experiment in 1990, a number of two-and-a-half mile maiden races for five-, six- and seven-year-olds only, were allowed. The horses were not allowed to be flat racing graduates, and any horse that had even run under N.H. rules carried an automatic penalty. The idea was to encourage young point-to-pointers (who might one day go on to be steeplechasers) without pitting them against speedy non-stayers from the professional ranks.

Setting about acquiring your first point-to-pointer can be so full of pitfalls that negotiating the three miles and eighteen fences of your first race is going to seem like child's play by comparison. It is so easy to flick a catalogue at an auction and next minute be the owner of a horse. Then you find out what's wrong with him...but many of his shortcomings should have been discovered beforehand. Afterwards, all too often, is too late.

At this juncture, a word about mares: a good many people will not buy a mare at any price. Although some mares will be too insubstantial and some may prove awkward when in season in the spring, this does not alter the fact that a good mare is generally a very good horse indeed and capable of reaping you plenty of reward.

The Need to Buy a 'Schoolmaster'

Firstly, remember the maxim 'never put two novices together'. As a new rider starting out, the most important thing is to acquire an experienced horse. This almost certainly means going out and buying one, because until he has shown his capability on the racecourse, the watching world is unlikely to offer a novice jockey a 'spare' ride.

Try and buy your horse by late summer or early autumn, so that you can get to know each other from scratch, building up together. If you buy a horse who is already racing fit, he will almost certainly be several steps ahead of you, but by starting off walking in the autumn, followed by a season's hunting, the chance of building up a good rapport with each other is that much greater.

It is essential to buy a 'schoolmaster', and by this I do not mean a slowcoach that never gets into the race, but a horse with experience, a safe record, and preferably some form.

The new rider does not want to be plodding round in the rear, but mixed up in the hurly burly of it all, so that he samples the thrills of racing and, after a race or two, will have learnt enough to have a real chance of winning. That, after all, is what it is all about.

By definition, a schoolmaster is not going to be very young, and a horse in his prime may prove too expensive unless there is something wrong with him, but there is really nothing wrong with a horse of twelve or even thirteen to get you started. The chances are that he will be fairly sound to have

4

reached that age and still be racing, and a horse of this type may prove to be a real bargain.

Sources of Information

So how to find this paragon? Not easy! The chief ways are at auction, through an advertisement (probably in *Horse and Hound*, *The Sporting Life*, *Racing Post*, or sometimes a local paper), or by word of mouth through a dealer or friend.

Whatever else, beg, borrow or buy a formbook; this is imperative. Failure to study the formbook in advance once left me with a horse who reared at the start of a race, shot off down a spur of the course, stopped dead and dropped me off! The resultant visit to the stewards' room elicited a heartfelt promise from me not to run the horse again — but his previous roguish behaviour had been in the 'book' for all to see.

For form under N.H. rules you need *Chaseform*; don't worry about form on the flat, as this is too far removed from the horse you require. Bear in mind that a horse who has been running in mid-division of big hurdle fields on grade one tracks may well be a better buy than one who has won a modest selling hurdle; the former may not only be a better horse, but will be eligible for maidens whereas the second type would be liable to carry a penalty in some races and would be ineligible for a restricted open as well as a maiden race.

The middle-of-the-range horse can either turn out to be expensive if your research has failed, or a bargain. Many horses in training become sickened of the game; they may have won in the past but have lost their enthusiasm and with it their form. This is where hunting can be a great tonic and can transform a jaded horse, rekindling his zest when racing between the flags.

In addition to *Chaseform* you will need a point-to-point annual form book. For many years, there was only one, *Hunter Chasers and Pointer-to-Pointers (19--)*, begun by Geoffrey Sale in 1960 (giving the 1959 season form), and although many of his comments on horses and riders were somewhat caustic, nevertheless most enthusiasts bought 'the book', which, although often used as a betting guide is also a record for owners and riders. Sale was joined by Iain Mackenzie, and when he retired from it, Mackenzie was joined first by David Phillips and then by Terry Selby, with whom he still produces it, *Horse and Hound* having been responsible for its publication between 1975 and 1983.

The *Sporting Life Point-to-Point Form and Results* has been published since the late 1980s and *Pointerform* is another annual. This is produced by David Coulton of *The Pointer*, a weekly form guide produced during the season and distributed either inside the racecard or on sale separately. Most areas now have a racecard form guide included, usually compiled by an expert within that area, such as Henry Franklin in the South Midlands who is also a regular commentator. Additionally, *Horse and Hound*, *The Sporting Life* and the *Racing Post* produce comprehensive weekly results services in their respective journals, so by keeping these it should be possible to have some idea of the true worth of a horse.

Remember, whether buying from the sales, or privately, to check that the horse is qualified for point-to-pointing. Not only will he be ineligible if he has run on the flat or under N.H. rules in or after the November immediately prior to your point-to-point season, but even if he has simply been on a trainer's monthly return.

Buying Privately

Decide what sort of price you can pay and try to stick to it; don't buy in a hurry; and if buying privately, always have the horse vetted. This can prevent wasting a lot of money on a 'wrong' horse, although my mother's best horse, Rough Scot, failed the vet as a four-year-old ('those hocks are too weak to stand cubhunting let alone racing'.) Mother, however, had a hunch about him, bought him for £400 (in the late 1960s), and he won her sixteen races; it helped that she already had some of the same family from his breeder, Peggy Pacey. To find a reliable source to which you can return over the years is a great bonus.

Buying privately has the advantage over auction sales of

your being able to ride the horse at his home to get the feel of him. Don't be satisfied with riding him round the field in which he has just been shown off to you (and always see someone else ride him first in case he does something dangerous, like bolting). Ask if you may ride away from the stables, on the road, and with and without company; ride the horse past the gate on the way home to see if he naps; and see if you can jump over something other than the fences he is used to.

Buying privately may be costly, but not necessarily so, and it is possible to pick up a bargain. One such was Daraheen Sniper, for whom Angela Howard-Chappell paid the sum of £1400 in the late 'eighties. He was a genuine schoolmaster, but to begin with, in her words, Angela 'kept falling off him'. It all paid off the day Angela recorded her third win on him, beating a horse reputedly bought for some £12,000 − and did it by sheer good riding. Daraheen Sniper, who was then eleven, was running in the fiftieth race of his career that day.

Sarah Dawson found her schoolmaster, Mr. Mouse, through the columns of *Horse and Hound*. She fell in love with him at first sight, but was advised by her vet not to buy him because of signs of previous leg trouble.

Sarah looked at others, but in the end bought 'Mouse' anyway, for just under £2,000. It was only once she got him home that she realised how little she knew herself; not only had she never ridden a thoroughbred before but she had never even hunted, and soon she found her purchase too much for her.

Reluctantly, she re-advertised him and had the good fortune to be contacted by point-to-point enthusiast Steven Astair who, with his trainer Chris Loggin, took both horse and rider under their wing in Northamptonshire. Unseated in her first ride on him, she ended the season with a commendable second − and felt much gratitude towards her unexpected benefactors.

In 1990, the winners of N.H. racing's two most prestigious steeplechases, the Grand National and the Cheltenham Gold Cup, had both not only started their careers between the flags, but had changed hands for modest sums of money.

Norton's Coin, the 100−1 shock Gold Cup winner trained on

a small dairy farm near Carmarthen, was the son of a £700 hobdayed miler and was sold locally when still 'in utero'. The 'book' said of him after his first season point-to-pointing: 'won a humble contest readily and may be able to make the transition to restricteds'.

Mr. Frisk's temperament was so suspect that it was a wonder he ever made the grade in point-to-points at all, let alone the 'National. He point-to-pointed for his breeder, and after winning four — when the 'book' reported that he was inclined to sweat up and be excitable in the paddock and was 'not the easiest of rides' — he was sold at Doncaster Sales for what was to prove a modest 15,500 guineas. He became a great credit to trainer's wife Tracey Bailey who used to lead him off her hunter for his cantering work. These were two fine examples of point-to-pointing being a nursery school for future N.H. horses.

Buying at Auction

If money is short when you are looking for your schoolmaster it will probably be best to go to the sales, and although this will be a gamble, the right horse can be found. Again, the form book is the biggest ally.

The two principal English sales at which to find a likely point-to-pointer are Ascot and Doncaster. Both are held in racecourse stable premises, Ascot being run by Messrs John and Michael Botterill from York, and held monthly and Doncaster being run from Hawick, with some of its sales being held over four days. There are also N.H. sales in Ireland but there prices tend to be high.

Do read through the conditions of sale, as little things can vary. Doncaster and Ascot, for instance, employ different forms of warranty: at Doncaster, a horse warranted sound has to be vetted on the premises on the same day by a sales vet for the horse to be returnable, while at Ascot, the purchaser has two days in which to have the horse vetted at home. At both sales, there is seven days in which to discover vices like windsucking, crib-biting or shivering, for which the horse is returnable.

Many trainers who are selling do not warrant their horses, but if buying one that is, make sure he is vetted within the time limit. Bear in mind also that a horse who is warranted sound is not absolved from nappiness; indeed, it often seems to be 'doggy' horses who take care to keep themselves sound, refusing all efforts to cajole them into any exertion on the racecourse.

Before sale day, study the catalogue, mark the horses that sound promising, then, after studying the form book, delete as many as necessary. Perusing the catalogue is a little bit like looking through details of a property for sale: you have to learn to read between the lines. If the size of a horse is not included, it is a fairly safe bet that he is not very big; similarly, a horse described as being suitable for a lady very often simply means that he is not big enough for a man. A horse advertised as 'placed in open company' is no doubt a truthful description, but how many runners were there in the first place? The horse may have finished a tailed-off third of three, and may even have fallen and remounted en route. It is what is *not* said that you have got to be on the look out for. For some reason, a horse described as 'a good ride for an amateur' is often a euphemism for a horse who has broken down.

On sale day, get there in plenty of time, and walk round methodically, beginning with the lowest number in your catalogue. Only if there is one that you really feel you must try and see first should you go out of order, otherwise you will end up with much sorer feet than you are likely to get anyway. Also, some of the later catalogued horses may not have arrived yet, whereas the earlier ones certainly should have done. You can reckon on roughly twenty-five horses being sold per hour, so don't go and miss one in the ring because you are still looking at others.

The first thing to do on arrival is check the list of withdrawals to see if any you have marked are included. Of the others, some you may dismiss on sight: too small, too weedy, or broken down. Don't waste time glossing over faults that are too major to ignore; move straight on to your next prospective purchase. When you see one that looks as though he warrants a further glance, give him a pat on the neck, then run your hands down his forelegs, looking for tell-tale signs of leg trouble.

Don't worry unduly if the horse has been fired (which will anyway become rare following its ban in Britain in 1991) so long as he has raced since and the legs feel cool and hard to your touch. Past leg trouble is often indicated by bowing of the tendon, and the same criterion applies even if it has not been fired. Also place your thumb and forefinger round each pastern to see if they measure the same; if one is bigger than the other, there may have been low tendon trouble there, too. Check to see if the front feet are a matching pair. If they are not, it may be that one has been more broken up at grass than the other, but it may be a sign of foot trouble such as navicular. Have a look at his hocks to see if he has curbs, and check all round for signs of splints. An old splint or bony growth away from the tendon should cause no trouble. Also, look in his mouth, not to tell his age (being a throughbred, this is indisputable) but for signs of wear on the teeth which may mean he is a crib-biter, or to see if he is parrot-mouthed, which could result in it being difficult for him to eat, and thus be a 'poor doer'. You will want a horse who eats well for his arduous season ahead.

Have him led out of the box by his handler and stood on level ground outside. Walk around him, taking in the picture as a whole, then ask for him to be walked away from you and trotted back past you. This is to see what his action is like, as well as his temperament — if he flings himself about all over the place or refuses to go back into his box, you may have to think twice about him. This is especially important if you will be looking after him yourself at home; you are going to be keeping him for fun, remember, not to be kicked into Christendom.

His action should be straight and level. If he 'plaits' (legs crossing each other) or 'dishes' (swings one or more feet outwards in a circular fashion) badly he may have difficulty coping with the demands of point-to-pointing, although I would not worry about these faults if only slight.

If you still like him, he seems up to your weight and appears to be of a kind temperament, then go away and come back to look at him again later, perhaps when he has reached the pre-parade ring. Try and find out from the vendor why he is for sale and what he is like at home, in the stable and in traffic; all sorts of excuses and promises may be put forward but you may be able to glean something worthwhile. If any of the above is beyond you, take a knowledgeable friend to the sales with you (and when viewing privately for that matter) — although don't totally ignore your own intuition.

Some horses you like will make too much money (in some cases, the likelihood of this will be apparent before the auction). However, if money is no problem it is of course, possible to buy a very expensive horse with good recent form, and I don't agree with those who say such a horse will teach a newcomer little or nothing because 'all he has to do is sit there'. A good horse will teach more, and better, than a bad one, but it will put pressure on a new rider to have the added burden of riding a probable favourite when he is just learning, and this may be some consolation if you cannot afford a horse you really like the look of.

Finally, don't buy for the sake of it. Having twice been underbidder one September only to go home disappointedly empty handed, it was at the next month's October Sales at Ascot that we secured Mister Tack, a horse who went on to win seven races, including two hat-tricks....

3

Where to Keep Your Point-to-Pointer

How and where you keep your point-to-pointer will depend largely on your professional, financial and personal circumstances. The choices are: to keep him at home; to keep him at full livery; to keep him on a do-it-yourself livery basis.

This book will deal mainly with training the horse yourself at home, but if you have a free choice it is worth weighing up the pros and cons of all options.

There have, for many years, been successful point-to-point livery yards, but in the last decade they have proliferated, due to the increased wealth and leisure time which has brought many more first-time owners into the sport who have neither the expertise nor the inclination to train a horse themselves.

A number of livery yards are virtually professional racing yards and indeed some proprietors in recent years have gone on to make the grade as licenced trainers, for example Richard Lee and Henrietta Knight.

In 1989, Caroline Saunders turned out a record twenty-eight point-to-point winners from her Northamptonshire yard, plus a further five winners of hunter chases, with eighteen of the twenty-four horses winning, an incredible success rate. Her owners came from many different walks of life. They included Mr. Frank Gilman, a farmer and breeder, owner and trainer of the 1982 Grand National winner Grittar (ridden by Caroline's amateur father, Dick); Richard Russell, an investment banker, and Michael Watt, Chairman of Tattersalls, both of them with home-bred horses; widow Mrs. 'Twink' Thompson; Philip

Mann, a farmer; Johnny Greenall of the brewery firm; the late Tom Regis, head of Asphaltic Roofing; Charlie Main, in furnishing and fabrics; and in partnership, Bob Scruton who works for Marks and Spencer in London and Steve Wilshire, a business consultant. Lolly's Patch, who won four races for Mr. Main, was bought cheaply at Ascot Sales, while Mr. Russell had bought Teaplanter, one of the most exciting young horses in the country, for a few hundred pounds as a yearling. None of them, says Caroline, cost 'crazy money'.

If you work full time, especially in a desk-bound job, full livery may be the answer; the horse will be trained to near perfection, he will be turned out for you plaited, shining, and on time both out hunting and at the racecourse; and you will not have to worry about labour shortages, what to feed, when to call the vet or blacksmith, or who will look after your horse when you are away.

Even with all this done for you, you will need to get yourself fit to do your horse justice (as will be discussed in a later chapter). You will probably be encouraged to ride out at weekends and to school your horse if you are going to be his jockey. You will also discuss an outline programme with the proprietor, but while you have only your horse to think about, he may have several other owners and their horses to consider too.

Check in advance what extras may be added to your monthly bill: these are likely to include shoeing, veterinary fees and transport but are unlikely to include clipping. There may be extra for a horse that has to be bedded on shavings or paper instead of straw.

The do-it-yourself option is most likely to apply if you do not own your own land or stable, and either don't want or can't afford full livery. It comes in various types: you may simply pay a rent for the use of a stable and water supply, and somewhere to store your fodder and kit. In this case, you would provide your own fodder and hay, do your own grooming, exercising and mucking out, and you will be visiting at least twice a day. Alternatively, this option may include a combination of any of these services, and the price will be reflected accordingly.

The great advantage of keeping your horse at home is the rapport you can build up with him, and the satisfaction you can feel for a job well done. If you employ a groom for some of the basic tasks you probably have the best of both worlds.

4

Basic Management

Initial Exercise

Assuming your point-to-pointer has been out to summer grass, or just recently brought up for the sales, you will probably want to start work on him in early September. This must be walking only to begin with, to gently condition his summer fat, and you must not feed too much hard fodder too soon. How long he walks depends much on whether he is a light-weight, active sort of horse who gets himself fit, or if he is a heavier, more sluggish type who will need longer. Also needing longer will be the horse who has had leg trouble in the past and must be taken slowly. You want your horse's legs to be as hard as iron for the rigours of the season ahead and there are no short cuts.

You also want to avoid getting saddle sores on soft skin, and you must not jeopardise his wind by galloping too soon, so patience is the answer all round: take things one step at a time and you will reap the dividends later.

If you are able to turn your horse out for an hour or two, it may do much to keep him happy and relaxed. He is going to spend several months in his stable, and a period out each day can be a tonic that a jaded ex-racehorse has not indulged in before. By starting this practice at the beginning of the season, you do not run the risk of him 'turning himself inside out' if suddenly offered the freedom of a field halfway through the season, and the risk of injury is consequently less.

Fundamental Health Checks

Among the autumn jobs to be seen to when your horse comes in are shoeing, annual innoculation, teeth rasping and worming.

SHOEING   Ensure in good time that you have a farrier lined up for the season as in some areas they are like gold-dust to find. Check with him how much notice he likes for a visit and whether he has a particular day of the week allocated for your area.

Don't leave the ordering of a new set of shoes until the current ones are paper-thin and could cut into a leg like a razor blade, or until the nail heads are protruding or you are nearly certain to lose a shoe and risk a sore or bruised foot. Incidentally, when it comes to racing, some owners shoe point-to-pointers with aluminium 'racing plates', but others stick to conventional steel because these last longer. If a horse has poor quality hooves, it may be better to avoid repeated re-shoeing with racing plates. It should also be noted that calkins on hind shoes — used to provide extra grip — must not be longer than a quarter of an inch (6.5 mm.). This is a safety measure to protect fallen horses and jockeys.

ANNUAL INNOCULATIONS   The time you give your horse his annual influenza and tetanus booster may depend on the previous dates in his passport, but if you can do it at the beginning of the season, this is ideal.

The 'flu jab is a prerequisite of point-to-pointing as it is part of the Jockey Club regulations governing the sport, and it is essential that no jab is so much as one day late even several years in the past, or you will be fined and the horse will not be allowed to run again until the matter has been rectified.

Don't miss out on the anti-tetanus jab just because it is not compulsory. Some areas are rife with the disease in the soil and it can enter a horses's bloodstream through the tiniest cut. It causes a frightening, usually incurable illness. Very often, the innoculation is combined with 'flu so that one jab covers both. It is perhaps worth pointing out that you, too, should keep up to date with anti-tetanus injections!

TEETH RASPING   While you have the vet out to give the innoculation and to sign the horse's passport, it is also wise to have his teeth checked. They will probably need rasping, and other possible problems such as wolf teeth can be noted and, if necessary, dealt with at the same time.

Some people have the vet check their horse's back, lungs and heart on this annual check-up, too.

WORMING   Another must is worming. Worm control in your horse is imperative, and your vet will advise you on a regular programme. Your horse must be wormed when he comes in from grass and again two weeks later to get rid of the residual worms which had only been eggs during the first worming. After that, six-weekly intervals will probably be advised. Worming is one of the most neglected aspects of stable management but should not be so. If more foals and yearlings were wormed there would be fewer deaths from colic caused by aneurisms in later years. Without an efficient worming programme, you may find yourself puzzled later in the season as to why your horse eats so much food yet seems 'ribby' and stary-coated. Subsequent poor performance on the racecourse is inevitable.

Common Racehorse Ailments

It would be as well to look at some of the common ailments that beset point-to-pointers.

VIRAL INFECTIONS   Viral infections are the most prevalent ailment, considerably outstripping tendon trouble. Watch out for those tell-tale signs: a little cough; not clearing up just one meal; one heap of diarrhoea or of solid faeces indicating constipation; more sweat than usual after work. Even if your horse seems fine the next day, you have had the warning and should not run him until a blood test has given him the all clear.

TENDON TROUBLE   This, when it comes, is more of a blow because it invariably means two years off the racecourse, a long time in a horse's relatively short career. Research at Bristol Veterinary College has shown that even with the most minimal of tendon trouble (that is, not even lame, but just a fraction of heat or touch of swelling), takes fourteen months to resolve itself fully.

This brings us to firing, an age-old tried and tested treatment for tendon strain (and also complaints such as spavins and splints) which was banned by the Royal College of Veterinary Surgeons in September 1991 for treatment of soft tissue on humanitarian grounds. Firing is the use of red hot brand irons scalding lines or pin points into the skin covering the horses's damaged legs to try and make the damaged tissues heal together strongly through the thickened scar tissue. Many people feel that because it is a superficial treatment on the skin it is not beneficial to the underlying damage. However, many trainers are aghast at the ban. After winning the Grand National with Seagram in 1991, trainer David Barons claimed to have a greater recovery rate with fired horses than with those who had received a tendon implant. Horse vets themselves feel that it is the young, inexperienced vets along with the 'scientific boffins' who have brought about the ban, rather than the older vets in equine practice who have the wealth of experience of horses with 'legs' and their treatments — and who, given the chance, would still fire tendons.

The most important thing about tendon breakdown is to give the injury time to heal, and I have even heard of firing being advocated in order to force an impatient owner to give his horse the time needed for the healing process.

COMMON CAUSES OF LAMENESS   After virus, which can cause a horse to miss a season, and tendon trouble, which may mean a two year absence, other common ailments are numerically insignificant by comparison. Sore shins, most common in young horses worked on firm ground, can cause some hold up, and foot abscesses are an often ignored cause of trouble, which may stem from their qualifying hunting, and be due to weak feet.

A chip fracture, especially of the knee or fetlock, can, once diagnosed, be easily remedied by minor surgery which need not incapacitate the horse for the whole season. Too often, however, when the horse is still lame after two weeks, the owner will turn him out thinking time will be the healer. In this case it will not, but if examined, perhaps x-rayed, diagnosed and operated upon, it need not be a long case.

Another foot problem occurs in the hoof capsule, with the soft tissue of the outer structure and the sole of the walls causing an imbalance of the foot.

Overreaches, caused by a horse striking into the heel of a forefoot with a hind foot, are generally quite minor and should not take more than about ten days to heal up; the dead tissue should be cut away and the wound should be kept clean; antibiotics should not be needed, but trouble sometimes stems from owners failing to stop infection by cleaning the wound properly in the first place. A horse striking or being struck into a tendon results in a tendon injury as bad as if it had broken down and sadly, therefore, the recovery period will be as long.

This brings us to the question of bandaging point-to-pointers. There is a myth that bandaging a horse for racing will help prevent his tendons from breaking down. This is not so, but bandages help prevent external injuries. However, if bandages wrinkled or slip they can cause tendon damage, as they can also do if applied too tightly, restricting the blood flow and causing the leg to swell. The consensus among vets is that bandages are not the best protection for racehorses, because there is no way of ensuring they will not slip. The best form of protection, used quite widely by the eventing fraternity, is the portaboot, of stiff resilient manmade fibre, heated in an oven and moulded to each individual horse's leg, held in place either by a sewn bandage or by an outer, conventional brushing boot. These do not slip, do not allow mud or grit to get in, and give an even, uniform pressure.

Horses who 'brush' behind, that is, the corner of one hoof brushes against the opposite inside leg, should wear brushing boots, and for those that give themselves 'speedy cuts', similar but very high up the leg, there is nothing wrong with putting on elastoplast for protection. To counteract this problem, people sometimes three-quarter shoe their horse behind but this is not recommended by vets. Instead, the farrier should allow the inside heel to grow, and then put on a full shoe with a feathered edge, creating correct hoof balance which should eliminate the problem.

AILMENTS ARISING FROM MISMANAGEMENT The most common ailments that are due to stable mismanagement are azoturia, colic, chronic obstructive pulmonary disease (C.O.P.D.), mud fever and cracked heels.

Azoturia, a bit like cramp, is also known as Monday morning disease, set-fast, or tying up. It usually occurs in fit horses in fast work and on hard food after they have had a day off. In many stables, Sunday is a day of rest, but if their hard food is not cut back, horses may get azoturia during exercise the next day, hence Monday morning disease.

If a horse is taken for a gallop on Monday having had a day off on Sunday but no corresponding reduction in protein, the muscle cells will still be full of stored food. Suddenly they are being required to provide energy (for the gallop) and they cannot cope; the muscles 'tie up' or 'set fast', making the horse appear very stiff, usually in his back, or unable to move at all. He will sweat, the back and hindquarters will feel very hard, he will run a temperature and he may pass, with difficulty, dark, strong-smelling urine. It is very painful for the horse and prompt veterinary attention is essential. The vet will give cortisone injections and sodium salicylate. For some reason certain animals are more prone to this problem than others, especially mares. It should go without saying that when recovered, your horse must not be given too much hard food too soon. Build it up gradually as his exercise is built up again.

Colic is a stomach ache, often acutely painful, causing the horse to sweat, to paw the ground, to swing his head and neck round towards his flank, and to roll a lot, generally showing great signs of pain and distress, and he will be unable to pass any faeces. Call the vet immediately; if you delay, matters could become serious, the horse may twist his gut and death will follow. The vet will give a laxative, antispasmodic drugs and tranquillizers which will help relax the horse, ease the pain, and allow the intestines to return to normal. Prevention of colic should be possible by keeping to regular feeding times and not giving huge feeds in one go; not feeding overdry food; and not feeding very new, green hay.

Chronic obstructive pulmonary disease is caused by the effect of stable dust on the horse's respiration and consequently on his performance. It has become apparent in recent years that a great many horses are allergic to hay spores, dust and fungi, which cause them to cough; if allowed to continue, permanent damage will be done to the lungs, the horse will become broken-winded and unable to breathe properly. The solution is simple, though a bit of a chore: all hay must be soaked for twenty-four hours; this causes the spores to swell so much that they cannot pass into the horse's lungs. You must also give him dust-free bedding, either of shavings or shredded paper; and you must make sure there is good ventilation, including a roof vent in the stable. Also, you should not travel him with straw on the vehicle floor or with dry hay. Before the start of each season the stable, including the roof and rafters, should be thoroughly cleaned out, washed and brushed down and disinfected. If the horse next door is stabled on straw, there should be no cracks between boxes. Also, the muck heap should not be placed too close to the stables.

Mud fever and cracked heels are similar to chapped hands or lips in a human. Pale-skinned horses, especially those with white legs are particularly prone to mud fever. Some soils produce it more than others. Half washing a muddy horse will compound the problem, and the mud fever may even spread along the belly and flanks, but it is in the heels and lower legs that it is usually found, and may even occur in a dry summer at grass. The horse can end up with wide open, painful cracks in his heels, causing swelling and lameness, and bleeding, scabby spots. It is a good idea to smear vaseline into the horse's heels before hunting *before* he has the problem. Another method of prevention is never to brush his muddy legs when wet, as you will be rubbing the mud fever in further. Either wash and dry thoroughly (you may use a hair dryer), or leave it until morning and then brush it off when dry. A horse suffering from mud fever should be stabled wearing bandages over gamgee to keep the heels warm and dry.

BACK PROBLEMS   These occur quite frequently and are often the cause of a puzzling loss of form until detected and corrected. If your horse feels one-sided or jumps crookedly, or if you find he is scuffing the toe of one hind foot but not the other, his back may be 'out'. This usually means a vertebra or a couple of vertebrae have become displaced. Have the back checked by your vet or chiropractor, who will usually be able to manipulate it back into place and after only a few days rest, your horse will be transformed into his old self.

Feeding

The question of feeding is more than anything else a matter of common sense; you cannot set hard and fast rules on quantity, as this will vary from horse to horse and on the amount of work he is doing. The essence is to feed as much high energy food as you can, but it must be stressed that feeding is an art as well as a science. Therefore, although there are some basic guidelines to follow, it is impossible to give a hard-and-fast chart for your horse's diet. He is an individual animal, not a machine, and he will have his feeding fads just as much as any human being. He may eat volumes and never put on much weight; he may happen to dislike nuts; he may prefer eating at night to during the day; he may bolt his food if fed late; or he may have an equable, placid nature and simply eat what is put in front of him when it comes.

What you *can* ensure is the quality. If you cannot afford the best fodder, you should not contemplate owning a racehorse. Also, there are various rules you *must* stick to: feed little and often; feed at regular times; make the transmission from soft to hard food gradually.

Build up the food over the months, playing it by ear as to how much he can take, so that by the time of his first race he is eating all he will take in best fodder without going 'over the top'.

The horse in his natural state is a grazer, and has a small stomach which does not take kindly to huge meals in one sitting, but once you have started on set feeding times you must stick to them, or when a late feed arrives at last he may wolf it down and get colic.

Someone may have told you that you should feed 20 lb. (9.1 kg.) of 'hard' food a day when racing, but yours may be the type of horse that finds 14–15 lb. (6.4–6.8 kg.) sufficient. If you try and force him to eat more, he will leave food in the manger and will end up being put off his food altogether. It boils downs to stockmanship, having an 'eye' and a 'feel' for what is right. Little and often is a sensible rule; if, after his evening feed, you find your horse's manger empty on your last check round, then give him another bowl of oats. It is also advisable to feed all food, including hay, and water at ground level, as this is how horses would have it in their natural habitat. Feeding with the head down also helps develop the 'top line'. Keep the mangers and water bowls free from bedding, droppings or mice, and sweep a corner clear on which to put the hay. You then have to hope that the horse does not scrape the hay into his bedding and make it inedible. If you do use a haynet, this must be strung up high, so that your horse cannot get a leg caught in it when rolling.

The time of day you feed does not matter so much as regularity. In other words, breakfast can be 6 a.m. daily or 8.30 a.m. daily, but not first one and then the other. Half an hour either side is permissible.

If you feed early, give sufficient break before exercising; at least one hour from when the feed is finished. Also, if you exercise first, do not feed the horse while he is still hot and 'wound up'; give him at least half an hour's break.

The choice of food is up to you; on the one hand, you can either buy fresh oats and barley from a local farmer, and supplement them with sugar beet pulp with molasses, fresh carrots, household salt and cod liver oil. Bran, however, should be kept to a minimum when feeding your point-to-pointer because it has an inbalanced calcium/phosphorus ratio and this may also cause azoturia.

On the other hand, you may prefer to buy proprietary brands of prepared fodder. A tremendous amount of research will have gone into these, to ensure they make up a balanced and nutritious diet and that they are free from any contamination that could show up positive in a Jockey Club dope test (any point-to-pointer is liable to be tested.)

Depending upon your horse's individual appetite, breakfast and lunch may be simply a bowl or two of oats (probably 2½ lb. [1.2 kg.] per bowl) at each, although, if your horse eats quickly, you should add chaff to slow him down. Let him have his hay after he has come in from exercise. Supper is the main meal of the day and should be fed about 5 or 6 p.m. This is where you go to town in making it tasty and appetising. In addition to the oats — perhaps three bowls, which has brought us up to between 12½ and 15 lb. (5.7−6.8 kg.) for the day —

you can also feed nuts and/or mix, both of which also contain protein, sugar beet with molasses (which must be soaked for twenty-four hours or it will swell up inside the horse's stomach) and perhaps, depending on the type of horse, a bowl of cooked flaked barley. Hot boiled barley once a week the night before a quiet day or day off is a good idea; twice a week during pre-Christmas hunting. Additives should include household salt (especially after the horse has been sweating), carrots sliced lengthwise, or apples as tasty extras, and cod liver oil. Mineral additives can also be given on veterinary advice, and many horses enjoy the addition of eggs or Guinness (although the latter should not be given just before a race, in case a dope test shows up positive!). You may find you enjoy giving these extras yourself, feeling it provides more variation to whet your horse's appetite, even though good quality proprietary nuts or mix are sufficient if you want to give only these.

Do not let your fodder go off or stale; keep it in an airtight and mouseproof container. Do not feed your horse when he is hot or tired. When he comes home from hunting or a race, give him a small warm mash, and a bigger feed later on; not too much, because you want to keep him 'on his feed' and he may be thinking of the day's excitement more than food.

Keep fresh water available at all times except when the horse is hot or before he is due to gallop. He is likely to drink 6−12 gallons (27−54 litres) of water a day, depending on the weather, his size, and whether he has dry or dampened food; over half his body weight is made up of water, and it maintains his body fluids, helps with digestion and maintains body temperature.

At the start of the season, do two small things: make sure you have someone you can ask to feed for you should you be called away or held up at work unexpectedly; and weigh the oats in your bowl so that you know, rather than guess, how much your horse is eating through the season.

Also, obtain the best possible hay you can. A rough 'rule of thumb' on the amount of hay to feed is approximately 70 per cent hay to 30 per cent hard food when the horse is in light work; about 50−50 in medium work and about 25 per cent hay to 75 per cent hard feed when in hard work. You should not feed new season's hay for a month or two — some say not until Christmas — as this can be another cause of colic.

Remember always to feed according to the work being done, and treat each horse as an individual; if your horse's work is cut back for some reason, and especially on a day off, you must reduce his food accordingly.

If your horse is normally a good feeder and he suddenly leaves some, cut back the amount for his next feed and don't give him hard work. This is especially tough on you if he is about to race; you have brought him to peak, he has been eating and working well and anticipation is running high — but all your efforts will be for nought if you run him when there is something, however little, amiss.

Grooming and Clipping

Grooming, or 'strapping' is important, as it helps to build up and tone muscles and to produce a shine; however, both these qualities should be apparent in a horse who is fed well and exercised correctly without much grooming at all! Among the 'musts' are to pick out the feet daily and after every piece of exercise, to brush off dried mud and sweat, and to at least 'do over' before exercise. However, although a beautifully brushed mane and tail will look nice, these are the things that can be left if time is pressing.

By about October you will want to clip your horse, either a full hunting clip leaving in the saddle and legs, or a trace or blanket clip. With any type of clip, you may decide to leave in the head if you feel the horse is very thin-skinned and needs to be kept warm.

By this time, he should have 'done' his roadwork and be ready for a little bit more. The ideal thing is to take him cub hunting, to introduce him to hounds in a quiet atmosphere and to make a gentle start on grass.

5

Hunting

Certification

It should be stressed that, in order to point-to-point, the horse *must* have been hunting, this sport being the raison d'etre of the other.

True, there are those who 'qualify' their point-to-pointers by trotting round on the roads, their riders' knees up under their chins, and not a trace of mud or bit of puff evident when everyone else has enjoyed a good run. These types are favourite targets for cartoonists, but there is nothing new about them indeed, nearly 150 years ago, R.S. Surtees, writer and creator of Jorrocks, remarked:

'In the early days of steeplechasing a popular fiction existed that the horses were hunters...grooms used to grin at Masters requesting them to note they were out, in order to ask for certificates of the horses having been "regularly hunted", a species of regularity than which nothing could be more irregular.'

The conditions of the Bedford Steeplechase, *circa* 1810 stipulated, however, that runners had to have certificates saying they had been in at the death of three foxes in Leicestershire. The organisers were rewarded with a crowd of 40,000 spectators.

Although the regulations have changed a little over the years, the emphasis is still that the horse should have been hunted 'regularly and fairly'. A certificate is issued by the Master, and the owner has to forward this to Weatherby's (the Jockey Club's secretariat in Sanders Rd., Wellingborough, Northants) before the horse may run.

The certificate used actually to require the Master to declare that the horse had been hunted 'regularly and fairly', which was generally interpreted as being out hunting at least eight times until at least 2 p.m. However, even this system does not prevent a rider from paying little more than lip service to it. Today, it is the owner who makes that declaration, the Master only signing that the horse 'has been hunted properly'.

Hunts vary on how they cope with qualifying; some issue books of tickets, one ticket having to be given in on each day's hunting. It is up to the rider to make himself known to the Master at the meet, and to state the name of the horse he is qualifying. The newcomer is best advised to have a word with the hunt secretary before the start of the season to see which system is used in his hunt. Other riders, or the proprietor of a point-to-point livery yard, will doubtless put you in touch with the local hunt secretary but, failing this, the relevant information can be obtained from *Baily's Hunting Directory* or the hunting issue of *Horse and Hound* (usually published during October).

Some hunts allow a reduced subscription to those qualifying a point-to-pointer, and this will be useful to you if you do not have the time to hunt all season or will find it hard to afford a full subscription. But with this method, you will only be allowed out for the set number of qualifying days and will not be able to hunt more, even if you want to. Often, it is advantageous to give your horse another 'look at hounds' after he has qualified, even once racing has started, to keep him sweet and fresh, but by this time it would not be advisable to give him a full or adventurous day. Thus, a drawback of the ticket system is that it does restrict your hunting, but if time and/or money is short, it will be very helpful to you.

Your hunter's certificate must be lodged, with the current fee (£22 plus V.A.T. in 1992), 'by noon on a Wednesday to enable it to be entered for point-to-points which close on and after the following Monday'. In other words, assuming you are aiming for a Saturday meeting whose entries close the previous Saturday (as is mostly the case), the certificate must have been registered some two and a half weeks before the meeting.

The only exception is if you are entering only for your hunt members race. You still need a hunter's certificate, but instead of registering it, you are obliged only to send it in to the point-to-point secretary along with your entry.

Also, with the exception of members races, the horse's name must already be registered with Weatherby's. Since, in this book, we are talking about a horse with previous experience we can safely assume this to be the case already.

The rider also has to have a certificate, but he brings this to the races on the day, so the details of that are explained later. Neither the owner, owner's colours, nor jockey have to be registered at Weatherby's for point-to-points, although they do for hunter chasing, which will be discussed in the final chapter.

The Etiquette of Hunting

If you have never hunted before, it is as well to learn some of the basic etiquette beforehand, although this really boils down to common sense and courtesy. It is also worth learning a little about basic practice and procedures in order, for instance, that you do not incur the displeasure of others by 'heading' the fox — although obeying instructions from the Field Master and hunt staff should makes such gaffes less likely.

Although you need not get carried away by preconceptions about hunting attire, dress neatly and sensibly; normally, a black coat, black silk over skull cap, white stock, light-coloured breeches and black boots will suffice. Use a hunting — not racing — saddle and *don't ride with your knees under your chin.* You can practise riding with shorter leathers and a racing saddle at home but, out hunting, they are uncomfortable, impractical and make you look ridiculous.

Try to give your horse a calm introduction and, especially if he tends to be excitable in company, always give yourself, other riders, and hounds, plenty of room. If you have any indication whatsoever that your horse may kick out through excitement or aggression, you must tie a red ribbon to his tail — although this does not absolve you from taking due care yourself. Do not allow your horse to barge through gateways or in queues for fences.

In short, remember that hunting is not organised primarily for the benefit of point-to-point qualifiers, and that you are out by permission. Do not think of qualifying as a chore, but learn to enjoy it both for its own sake, and for the advantages that it can bring to the training process.

The Training Advantages and Other Pleasures ___

Although you have got your horse chiefly to point-to-point, you want, as an amateur, to enjoy him for the rest of the time as well, and while there are always risks, I believe the rewards of hunting your point-to-pointer properly easily outweigh them.

Hunting, of course, will not give you the 'feel' of racing, nor will it get either you or your horse racing fit, but it will help towards the overall goal. Instead of going straight from road work into fast work for racing, the horse has an extra two months in which to get fit gradually, at the same time finding an added interest and stimulation in life. Often it is also just the tonic a jaded ex-racehorse needs. Variety is the spice of life, and for the horse who has been a moderate, nameless number in the bottom yard of a big racing stable, the change of scene to hunting, point-to-pointing, and the individuality and informality (but not sloppiness) of a small, amateur yard can transform him.

The horse who has always gone out on smooth ground in a string of racehorses will learn to pick his feet up crossing difficult terrain, to extricate himself from difficulties and to jump 'trappy' places and ditches as well as fences. (If he has only ever brushed through hurdles or steeplechase fences in the past, it is worthwhile schooling him over low but solid timber at home before you hunt him.)

If you are lucky he will learn to queue, to wade across water, to negotiate a steep bank with small steps instead of huge leaps, and to keep his head generally in the hubbub and hurly-burly of the hunting field, so that the regulation of point-to-pointing in the spring is going to seem like a piece of cake by comparison!

He will also love the changing scenery, the sights and sounds of the countryside. It is rewarding when you notice your horse suddenly prick his ears and stare at something — you follow his gaze and there is the fox.

Naturally I do not advocate taking unnecessary risks and, in this context, it is worth remembering that riding carelessly on a metalled road — especially if it is frosty — can be more risky than taking on a big fence. However, as long as you are sensible and use your head and eyes, you will be unlucky to encounter serious injury and any minor ones should be patched up in good time before racing.

Very often, a thoroughbred will take a strong hold out hunting, and it may be necessary to change his bridle. To sail past everyone to the consternation of the Masters is an experience not unknown to me, but if a point-to-pointer is up in the first flight of a good hunt, along with the good jumpers, he will gain tremendous enthusiasm as well as experience, and that will be invaluable later on.

Occasionally, you will find a racehorse who simply will *not* jump timber, and there is nothing you can do about this. I once had one who was a superb fencer in point-to-points, but who could not be persuaded to pop over a 2 ft. rail! But many other great steeplechasers have retired to the hunting field and thereby extended their working life by many years; one such was Crisp, beaten hero of the unforgettable Grand National duel with Red Rum, and he spent several happy seasons in retirement hunting with the Zetland.

If you do find yourself with a horse who really is a hopeless hunter, then the only thing to do is get the qualifying over with as quickly and quietly as possible, and look forward to the training preparations.

6

Training the Horse

Facilities

Unless you are a landowner yourself, or have your horse at a livery yard with gallops, a farmer is probably going to be your best friend and ally over the next few months, for it is he who you hope will allow you to canter round his big old pasture field, or slip up the side of that steep bank he has, or use his tracks for trotting on. If he is one of the few left who grows spring corn and therefore still has stubble in the winter, so much the better, as stubble makes lovely cantering ground and the horse can do no damage to the land. With luck, the farmer will take an interest in the horse and even come to cheer him on at the local meeting.

Early Work

Training begins the day you bring your horse in during early autumn. We have already looked at the stable management jobs you must look to, now we must consider the exercise. You should begin by walking your horse under saddle daily; draw up the girths slowly and gently, or he may 'explode' after his long summer holiday. It may also help if you fit a roller to him for a few nights beforehand. Ride for only half an hour the first few days so that he does not get girth galls or a sore back. It will be very beneficial if he can also spend some time each day in the field, so that the change from being at grass to being stabled is a gradual one.

After a few days, increase the exercise to an hour, but still at the walk. Right from the start, try and vary your daily route. You will get bored with the initial chore of road work and so will your horse, so variety is the answer. Walk on the roads so that you do not encounter rough ground, so that your horse's legs will be hardened up, and so that your horse may not be tempted to buck and squeal on grass. Take in tracks as soon as you can and after a week walk around grass fields so that when you do come to do your first steady canter in about six weeks time he does not 'turn himself inside out'.

After about two weeks, include gentle trots and build up the length of daily exercise to about one and a half hours. Steady uphill work will benefit his lungs as well as his legs. After four weeks, you will notice that he is losing his 'softness', and his neck will begin to feel quite firm to the touch. His quarters, too, will be muscling up.

At about six weeks, take him for his first steady hack canters; do this preferably on a track that he has been trotting on so that he does not get too excited about it. It will now also be all right to take him out cub hunting, as you are unlikely to do any galloping or jumping, and the change of scene will do him good.

There is no need to give a horse a day off each week; this is usually done for the benefit of the humans concerned. If he does have a day off, try at least to get him out in the paddock, or led out in hand for a walk and a pick of grass for ten minutes. Reduce his feed, and make sure he has light exercise ther next day.

By the time he has done six to eight weeks preparatory work, he is ready to go hunting, and this will take you through to Christmas, having at least eight days out. The day after hunting he should be led out in hand, the next day taken for a walk and trot, and then let him have a quiet canter before his next day's hunting.

Building Up to Racing

One of the greatest joys in building up to racing itself is to have your horse taking just a decent hold beneath you in his exercise at home, his neck bulging with muscles so that the width of it in front of the saddle is considerably more than when you started together in the autumn. He tosses his head as you pat his neck and feel how hard it is. You know a transformation is beginning, and the real thing cannot be far away...

Take Boxing Day as a starting point for serious training of both your horse and yourself (for which, see the next chapter). This allows the weight-conscious rider one last blow-out at Christmas and leaves about the right amount of time before the point-to-points start in February to bring your horse to his peak.

His legs should be hard from his roadwork in the autumn and his condition should be 'hunting fit' after his qualifying. Now to lose excess fat, to condition and tone up his muscles until they are hard and rippling, and to clear his lungs. More than ever now, make sure he is not exposed to dust.

Keep up the roadwork, preferably taking different routes, but start taking in canters on grass several times a week, gradually increasing both speed and distance.

There can be no hard-and-fast training rules, common sense and individual horses again being the best pointer. The only criteria are that your horse should arrive at his first point-to-point fit and well-schooled, not fat. One of the reasons for record breaking N.H. trainer Martin Pipe's great success is that he gets his horses properly fit at home, instead of 'running them fit' on the racecourse. Seldom can it be said that a horse of his 'needed the race'.

Having said that, however, you must be equally careful not to 'leave the race on the gallops', by overgalloping him. Get him fit, but also keep him fresh, so that when it comes to raceday he is raring to go. Build up the work gradually, and above all with a jaded horse, try not to let him know he is actually working. For example, a horse only used to working on the wide open spaces of, say, Lambourn or Newmarket, will revel in hacking through the woods, along old railway lines and up the forestry plantation rides, and will simply not realise he is working at all.

By Christmas, you should have a good knowledge of your

horse; whether he is an active sort who gets himself fit or whether he is a lazy or thick-winded individual who needs plenty of work.

You will probably have met other point-to-point people out hunting and, if yours is a lazy horse, now is the time to see if you can sometimes work your horse with theirs, the competition of another horse alongside goading him to work better. Intersperse the long, slow canters with occasional short, sharp bursts, preferably uphill; these are marvellous as 'pipe-openers' to clear the lungs.

Once you begin to do faster work — and certainly before you race — you should master the technique of 'bridging' or 'double bridging' your reins. This is something you may not have done before. The idea is that if you let go of a rein with one hand, you have still got it safely with the other, and pressure is even on both reins. A 'double bridge', when both hands have got hold of both reins, gives you extra security when riding a hard puller, but a drawback of this is that if you cling on too rigidly and the horse makes a mistake you may be pulled over his head because you have not slipped the reins.

Don't forget that as you increase your horse's work you should also be increasing his hard food, and reducing his hay intake correspondingly, but always make sure he has some hay. By the time he is racing, he should be eating 15—20 lb. (6.8—9.1 kg.) of hard food per day, depending on the individual. Also, you should now be 'strapping' him really well daily.

Your next ally is going to be a local trainer; it will help enormously if you can have your wind-up gallop on his facilities, probably in return for a bottle of whisky or a fee. This gallop wants to be between a mile and a half and two miles long (never the full three miles of a point-to-point), should preferably include an uphill pull, and should be in the company of another horse. Do not gallop flat out. Have the horse 'on the collar' (with a taut rein, with the horse taking a firm hold of the bit) all the way, letting the reins out a notch as you gradually increase the pace until you reach 'three-quarters speed'. If he comes off the bridle, shorten your reins a little, give one slap down the shoulder to see if he is being lazy, but if he fails to take hold of the bit again, ease him up and acknowledge that

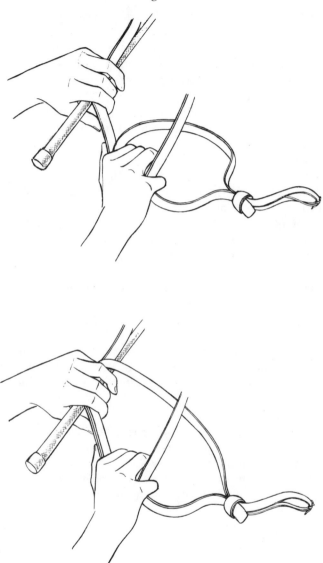

Bridging and double-bridging the reins

he is not as fit as you thought he was. If you continue, you run the risk of breaking him down or of distressing him. You are then going to need to give him a second gallop about a week later (depending on how he is eating and feeding at home) and if necessary you may have to put back the date of your first race a week.

On the other hand, if he finishes the work well, blows hard but does not take a very long time to recover, then you are 'on song', and you *must not* give him another gallop before the race, due in ten days to two weeks time.

One way in which point-to-pointing differs from steeple-chasing is the brevity of its season, four cramped months from February to May, and so the point-to-pointer will be running more frequently than his N.H. counterpart, usually fortnightly and quite often weekly. If follows, therefore, that he is not going to want much galloping at home, especially once he is racing.

You will, of course, give him some canter work two or three times a week between his wind-up gallop and the first race. Two days before his race give him a short, sharp pipe-opener and then do very little with him the day before, keeping him fresh. With a thick-winded horse it may be desirable to give him a leg stretch on the morning of the race. By this time he should be bursting, and you pray that it does not snow!

Dealing with Adverse Weather Conditions _____

A freeze-up in January or early February can hold up training preparations considerably. If you have deep snow, you will be able to work in it, slowly, and your horse will love it, snorting his pleasure.

If what you suffer, though, is severe frost, making the land unrideable, then you are going to need your trainer again, for permission to use his all-weather gallop. Increasingly, amateurs make use of these, not only during a freeze-up or when the ground is very heavy but for 'ticking over'. However, I still feel there is a danger of a horse getting bored, and if you can do the same job but with greater variety around a plantation, then so much the better. Indeed, if you can reach the sea, this is another wonderful change of scene for your horse and especially useful during a freeze-up. Even from the Midlands it is well within the bounds of possibility to reach Burnham-on-Sea, south of Bristol, to canter along the sands.

This is a spot that professional trainers also use, but whichever beach you go to, you must ensure in advance that the sands are safe. Camber Sands becomes a mecca for stables throughout Kent and Sussex at such times, but I remember once arriving there to find a dense sea fog which made cantering extremely hazardous. Also, sand is notorious for having soft patches in it which, if hit at speed, may cause a horse to break down. Alternatively, it can be so firm that it rattles like a road, and so the safest rule is to use beaches for steady canters and not as gallops, unless like Red Rum's trainer Ginger McCain at Southport, you harrow a strip along the sands to work on.

There are no hills for pulling up on a beach and I remember once riding a horse who was taking such a hold I headed into the waves to try and pull up, but it was a most uncomfortable experience and not to be recommended.

Schooling Over Fences

Schooling must be neither neglected nor overdone. We are talking about an experienced horse and a novice rider, so the schooling is going to be more for the rider than the horse, although for the horse it will put his eye in and limber up his jumping muscles. The chief advantage to schooling over fences lies in the speed of jumping, because you never jump at racing pace out hunting, and to be happy in a race, you must first have schooled. The schooling will enable you to adjust to jumping fences at near racing pace, something you have never been confronted with before, not even in a team chase. It is the speed of racing which is one of its biggest thrills.

The schooling should be two or three weeks before your planned first race. Any earlier, and you may 'rev' your horse too much in advance of the race, any later, and you run the risk of an irritating small overreach not healing in time, or of not having enough time left for a second school should that seem necessary. The fences in point-to-points have to be 4 ft. 3 in. (1.3 m.) high, only 3 in. (8 cm.) lower than their N.H. counterparts, and include an open ditch. A very few courses, like Tweseldown and Kimble, include a water jump (with a smaller fence on the take off side). A course inspector is appointed for each course, and the whole sport is closely controlled by the Jockey Club, under whose jurisdiction it falls.

Your schooling fences should be slightly smaller replicas of point-to-point fences, made of birch, not flimsy, and inviting. If you use thin fences or ones with holes in, you will court disaster; the horse will not jump properly and will be in for a rude awakening when encountering fences on the racecourse. The schooling fences must be wide enough to accommodate at least two horses with room to spare, and must have good wings. They should be sited on well drained ground, preferably slightly uphill, and should be two or three in a row, the last one an open ditch. If you do not have the facilities yourself, again it is going to be a matter of paying a tenner to a local trainer to hire his.

It is a good idea to put boots on your horse for schooling, and don't forget to check the drawstrings inside your crash cap: they must be adjusted so that there is a cushion of air between the lining and the skull cap itself.

It is essential to school with another horse, an experienced one and not one who is going to run out or refuse! In fact, it is vitally important that the schooling takes place in a calm, controlled manner. Trying to go schooling with Hooray Henrys ends up more frightening than the race itself. You want to follow the other horse the first time, and go upsides him the second time, to give you some idea of the 'feel' of jumping at speed in company.

One of the trickiest situations to avoid in a race (and schooling) is being 'half-lengthed' at a fence. This is where one horse is only half a length ahead of you, which can result in your horse having his eye distracted and being tempted to take off when the other horse does instead of putting in an extra stride. This is often the cause of a fall, so you must try and be either upsides a horse or one length behind.

Being half-lengthed

It may be a good idea to have your first school over a couple of flights of hurdles, to get your eye in and get some taste of jumping at speed, but over smaller obstacles.

Before you school, have a 'breeze up' somewhere, walk to where the schooling fences are, show your horse the first fence, and walk back to where you intend to start, probably about fifty yards; it does not have to be as far back as in the start of a point-to-point.

The horse knows what is up, and may be jogging and eager to get on with the job, so you must be ready yourself. For perhaps the first time, you will experience a few butterflies in your stomach: after months of steady preparation, the real thing is approaching.

Before turning him, shorten your reins (not too short or you may be pulled over his head if he makes a mistake), have the reins in a 'single bridge', then turn and surge off. Keep a straight line, keep to the middle of the schooling fence, and if following another horse, keep two to four lengths back.

You should not school at full racing speed, but you should go fast enough to get some idea of what it is all about. If you are lucky, your experienced horse will measure his fences perfectly, and you will soar over.

You must not 'showjump' over fences, or you will fall off

Approaching and jumping a point-to-point fence: *a) correct approach*

should your horse peck on landing. This is because of the speed and type of fence involved. The schooling must be conducted at such a pace that the horse is allowed to quicken the last three strides, therefore the correct schooling pace is comparatively steady, allowing the horse to lengthen his stride for the last three strides into the obstacle. The seat adopted by the novice is often determined by his size, but try and keep yourself neat and tidy. Try not to hang on to your horse's mouth but go with him, but at the same you must learn to slip your reins, and to put your lower legs forward to take the

3

4

weight and help prevent you from falling off if the horse makes a mistake. You also need to learn to lean back from the waist in case of a major blunder.

Although you may be little more than a passenger to begin with, this is better than flapping about all over the place. Nonetheless, it is sensible to give your horse some assistance going into a fence so, without exaggerating it, use your seat and squeeze with your legs. You are only likely to have to kick if you have a very lazy horse; sometimes a slap down the shoulder is just the encouragement he needs.

A mental 'one, two, three' as you approach the fence should ensure the two of you go over in unison but *don't* 'hook back'

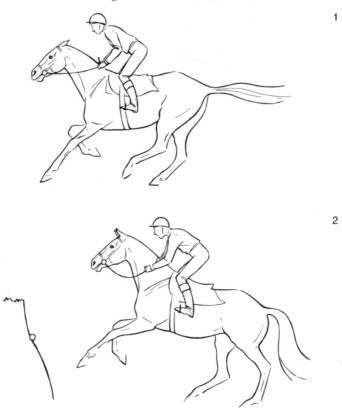

Approaching and jumping a point-to-point fence: *b) incorrect approach*

to try and get the stride right. This is one of the biggest differences between fencing in a race and any other type of equestrian jumping.

Instead, if you are 'all wrong' approaching a fence, either sit still and let the horse fiddle it while you mentally prepare to alter your centre of balance in order to keep in the saddle, or 'ask' him for a long one, and hope he responds!

A couple of schools should be quite sufficient for your horse; too much schooling can lead to unnecessary mishaps.

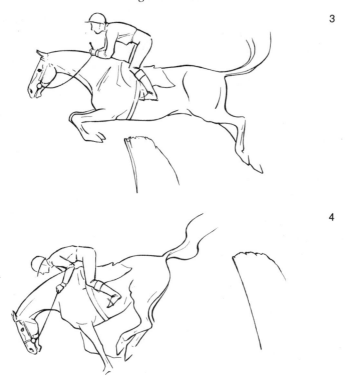

3

4

(With a young horse, it is different. 'Schooling in public' is not only against the code of point-to-pointing, it is downright dangerous not only to the horse and his rider, but to all others in the race, too. Therefore, a novice horse will need to be jumping telegraph poles at Christmas, followed by bushed up flights of hurdles, then miniature fences before schooling fences of about 4 ft. (1.2 m.). At each stage, the young horse must be led over the fence first by an experienced horse, then must jump it upsides another horse, and then lead over it himself before progressing to the next height at a later date.)

Occasionally you will get a wily old horse who simply won't

school; if this is the case with your horse, and you know he is a good jumper of fences on the racecourse, don't worry about it too much; he will be the sort who can be relied upon to look after himself (and therefore you) when racing. If you can persuade a friend to let you have a school on his old horse, then so much the better.

Practise, of course, is difficult for the new rider to come by, accepting that his horse does not want to be either overgalloped or overschooled, and no amount of schooling will give you an insight into your first race; but there are ways of getting yourself as fit to race-ride as possible, both physically and mentally, before the big day...

7

Training Oneself

The Need for Physical Fitness

It is no use having trained your horse to perfection for the first race if you, yourself, are not fit enough to do him justice. Not only must your muscles be strong but, just as with the horse himself, your wind must be clear: galloping at 30 m.p.h. on a freezing February day can send a searing pain through your chest if your lungs are not prepared for an intake of piercing Arctic air.

It is going to take a lot of willpower to get yourself fit, especially if you have a sedentary job. Age also comes into the fitness question and, for the older person embarking on point-to-pointing, the need to get fit is even greater, and the process even harder. That said, even a basically fit, healthy young person should not ignore the need to get into proper racing trim.

Everyone has their own tortuous methods of getting fit, but two chief allies are needed; a friendly, helpful racehorse trainer and one's own determination.

When embarking upon your fitness programme, Boxing Day is the latest practical starting point − and it is also an appropriate date if weight loss is to be involved! Although you will be hunting fit by that time this, in no way, is racing fit − for a start, different muscles will be called into play. You may sit in the saddle for five hours out hunting, but your seat will be out of the saddle for the six minutes of a race, your weight will be placed differently, and everything will happen more quickly.

Riding Out

If you can ride out for a local trainer on a regular basis this will not only help you from a fitness point of view, but will assist greatly in savouring the general feel of riding racehorses, getting used to their idiosyncrasies, and being mentally attuned to them.

It will give you much needed practise in riding work, in 'sitting against' a horse, in having him 'on the collar', in noting the different speeds, learning to hold a puller, and riding shorter than you would do out hunting. Incidentally, don't worry too much about riding a puller in a race; a horse who pulls your arms out at home will be going that much faster in a race so that, barring the exceptional few, you won't find it a problem. Indeed, just the opposite, for it will be easier for you to sit against such a horse than to ride one who needs pushing and shoving along.

To get used to riding shorter, it is unwise to pull your leathers ('jerks') up too much or too soon; do it gradually, a hole or two at a time, so that your muscles attune gently. Don't make the mistake of riding as short as a professional jockey when embarking upon your point-to-point career; have your leathers short enough to help you distribute your weight in a racing seat but long enough to be comfortable.

If you can ride first lot with a trainer before going to work, so much the better, but if you only have time to exercise your own horse, which will mean not much fast work, then practise trotting with your seat out of the saddle. Take hold of the martingale neckstrap so that if (or when) you lose your balance, instead of jobbing your horse in the mouth, the neckstrap takes the pressure. This should also prevent you plomping down in the saddle too heavily. This exercise will help strengthen your thigh and lower back muscles, and similar benefit can be derived from riding a bicycle without a saddle.

Basic Fitness Techniques

If your horse is strong you may find that even your fingers, as well as your arms, get stiff. Squeezing a small rubber ball will help your fingers and wrists and has the advantage of being something you can do virtually anywhere — even when stuck at traffic lights while driving a car. One way of strengthening your arms and wrists is to hoist yourself up off the ground from bannisters, although you may prefer to use a gym.

With fitness and work-out centres being so popular now, you are bound to have one within fairly easy reach. There you can 'run', 'cycle' and 'row' to your heart's content on different machines. Aerobics, another name for doing exercises to music, has also caught on, with many towns holding weekly sessions, which really do help with overall fitness.

Running, cycling and swimming are some of the best forms of exercise to take, running in particular also helping with the wind. You will find yourself doing long, steady jogs, and short, sharp uphill pipe-openers just like your horse! The hardest part of going for a run is starting it. After a while, you engage 'automatic', settle into a rhythm, and before you know where you are you are actually enjoying it!

Expert Advice — A Case History _____

Some people look to a fitness expert for advice; Charlotte Brew did this before she became the first woman to ride in the Grand National in 1977; Keith Allison, a physical trainer, watched her ride her horse at work to note which muscles were most important and from there devised a routine to develop them in his gym, making use of weights, and also swimming and running. Smoking and drinking were strictly out, and boyfriends were not encouraged, either.

In 1988, Hampshire-based Amanda Hamilton-Fairley, who had point-to-pointed for a few years, decided to take her own training more seriously, and enlisted Olympic athletic coach Frank Dick to help her:

I had ridden all my life, and graduated from Pony Club to eventing, but it was not until I turned my hand to point-to-pointing that I ever thought of my own fitness as something to be considered separately from that of my horse.

Frank Dick, also personal coach to decathlete Daley Thompson and involved with tennis star Boris Becker, devised a fitness plan to suit a point-to-point rider — and made a 'new woman' of Amanda.

A stockbroker with a 9 to 5 job in London, Amanda admitted that previously she had only paid lip service to getting herself fit, going to a gym two or three times a week to work out on weight machines and exercise bikes. 'There was no systematic approach and therein lay my fundamental mistake, as I was soon to find out,' she says.

Rule number one, Frank told her, was to plan her day to allow enough time for exercise, even if this meant getting up earlier, or giving up a lunch hour, or finding the time at home instead of just collapsing after work. His second rule was not to expect to find it easy — it was hard work and total commitment that won Becker Wimbledon, not a wing and a prayer...

To build up general strength and endurance, he advised running, but again this was to be no hit-and-miss affair, but based upon carefully devised schedules. To begin with, Amanda jogged (slowly) for four 5-minute sessions with 1 minute walk in between; this built up to four 7½ minute sessions, still with 1 minute walk in between. From there she progressed to 25 minutes continuous running. Interspersed with this she was doing sprints, sprinting for 15 seconds, jogging for 45 seconds, beginning with twelve repeats and increased to twenty. After this, she embarked upon uphill sprints of 200 metres and jog down, repeated four times, and then again after a 3 minute break.

Finally, Frank gave her the target of completing a particular cross-country run in 30 minutes. Imagine her feelings when, on returning in 31½ minutes, he immediately sent her out again to achieve it within the designated time; 29½ minutes later, elated rather than exhausted, a triumphant Amanda returned!

All this revolved around basic fitness; now specific areas were targeted: to enable her to hold a particularly strong horse, Frank put her on to arm-circling exercises, lying face-down on the floor, arms outstretched in front, then lifting them off the ground and circling them ten times clockwise, ten times anticlockwise, repeating to the sides, and then behind the back. Half a minute's rest was allowed, with the process repeated three times, before progressing to doing the same exercise with weights in each hand. This built up the muscles in her arms, shoulders and the base of her neck.

Other exercises involved skipping (forwards, backwards, sideways and swinging hips from side to side); bunny hops; and exercises in water. The latter included treading water for 15 seconds vigorously followed by 15 seconds slower, the process repeated four times, and then again after rests for four or five times more. This, Amanda said, worked wonders for developing the strong thigh muscles needed for riding short. There were also water exercises in which she wore a weighted jacket, running through the water for 20 minutes.

In a final move to attain the total fitness required to ride in a steeplechase, Frank devised the 'Power Run'. In this, a 30 second sprint was followed by a series of exercises representing the motions of jumping a fence and then, after a 20 second sprint, the exercises were repeated, followed by a 10 second sprint, and the exercises again. The whole was repeated, with the final 10 seconds representing the run to the line. After a rest of 3 minutes, the whole process was repeated.

It is hardly surprising that when the point-to-point season opened that February, there were few, if any, amateur riders fitter than Amanda!

She adds:

The whole thing was fun, and had the added benefits that I lost considerable weight and felt both healthier and stronger. It helped my racing enormously, I could ride three races in an afternoon and my position improved, it was much tidier.

Being physically fit and feeling well and strong has the added benefit of helping your mental attitude — believing in yourself and in your ability to win a race means you can be more adept at making your own opportunities or capitalising on opportunities that arise during a race. There's no need to discuss the psychology of winning in any detail but self-confidence can and does grow with physical fitness and there is no doubt that self-confidence can help you to succeed.

Slipping the reins

Practising Racing Techniques

One of the difficulties of being a one-horse owner/rider embarking on point-to-pointing is lack of 'match practise'. Nothing substitutes for the real thing, and while riding out for a trainer will help no end, even there, opportunities will be limited. You cannot expect to ride 'work' (that is, canter or gallop), every time you go there, and you are unlikely to school any horses at all other than your own.

Nevertheless, there are little racing techniques you have to master if you can. One is to move your lower leg forwards over a jump, which you would not normally do if you were showjumping. The other is slipping the reins.

For the jumping practise, I used to commandeer the family cob, and jump him over a small drop hedge. While not giving the same 'feel' as a racehorse, it was nevertheless the ideal method for mastering getting those lower legs forwards – and, of course, the cob loved it, just as he did when mustered as 'lead horse' over the schooling fences.

Slipping the reins is another technique which can be practised, on a cob over a drop fence. Just ease your fingers off the reins as you are in mid-air, allowing the reins to let out a few inches (much as you let out line while playing a fish) and close them again as you land. Having done this, you then have to practise 'picking up' the reins and shortening them again, as smoothly and precisely as possible.

8

The Whip

The whip and its use in racing are emotive and often mis-understood topics and, unfortunately, there are some people who do not think they have ridden in a race unless they have spent some time flailing around like demented windmills. It is as well, therefore, to devote some time to examining this subject.

The Jockey Club Point-to-Point Regulations specify the type of whip allowed, emphasise the powers of the stewards regarding the use of the whip and define both improper use and correct use of it.

The whip itself must be no longer than 30 inches (76 cm.) including the flap and have a minimum width of 5/16 inch (8 mm.) The flap must be no longer than 4 inches (10 cm.) and must be a minimum of ¾ inch (2 cm.) wide.

The Jockey Club has the good sense to define what they consider to be the correct use of the whip: hitting horses on the quarters or, with the whip hand on the rein and the whip in the backhand position, down the shoulders; showing horses the whip before hitting them; using the whip in rhythm with the horse's stride; using the whip as an aid to keep a horse running straight; keeping the whip hand below shoulder height. It adds that in all races the number of deliveries of the whip used on a horse which is answering to encouragement should be limited to a minimum.

Regarding abuses of the whip, the Jockey Club defines un-necessary use as continued hitting of horses which are clearly winning and of hitting horses after the winning post.

Misuse, it states, is hitting horses in a wild manner thus unbalancing and impeding progress (perhaps the most common fault of the novice rider); hitting horses with a degree of severity which injures; hitting horses in any place other than on the quarters or down the shoulders with the whip in the backhand position 'except in very exceptional circumstances' and hitting or appearing to hit horses with unreasonable force or frequency.

Excessive use is defined as excessive hitting of horses which are responding under the whip regardless of their final placing; repeatedly hitting horses over a short distance having no regard to their stride pattern (another minefield for the novice rider); persistent hitting of horses which show no response under the whip; and continued hitting of obviously beaten horses or 'similar instances'.

Without specifying precisely, stewards are likely to look into cases where the whip has been used more than ten times since the penultimate point-to-point fence; where the horse has been marked in the wrong place; where the whip has drawn blood; and if the number and severity of the weals are such that the vet considers the horse has been injured.

Owners are reminded of their responsibility for giving instructions to riders including use of the whip, especially with thin-skinned horses, and it is within the stewards' powers to take disciplinary action against owners who fail to give adequate instructions or give instructions which if obeyed could or would lead to a violation of point-to-point instructions.

All this may seem obvious and common sense, but it is surprising what can happen when the blood is up; at all times, try and keep a clear head.

The novice rider would, in fact, be well advised to avoid using the whip altogether until he has some experience of race-riding.

In the initial stages, the best thing is to practise how to 'pull it through' while out walking, and how to apply it from on top of a saddle horse — definitely not on a real horse. The transition from passive to active position of the whip is simply a matter of practise and dexterity, a bit like one learns different grips on a tennis racquet — with a flick of the wrist, a change of the

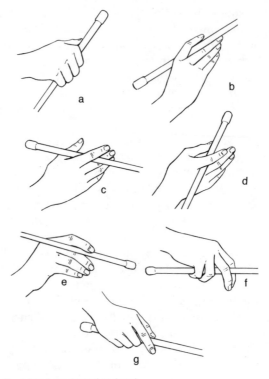

Changing the whip from 'carry' to 'use'

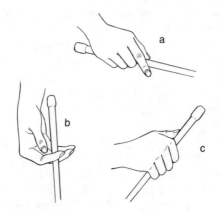

Changing the whip from 'use' to 'carry'

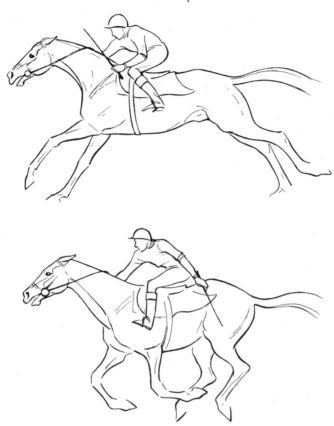

Using the whip correctly in rhythm with the horse

fingers and then of the thumb, hey presto it is ready for action.

If you do plan to use the whip in a race, it is best just to 'swing it' once or twice first, as this may be enough to 'sharpen up' the horse. If you apply it, keep it parallel with the side of the horse (don't stick it outwards and thump the horse inwards), and having got it into a swinging rhythm — forwards as your hands go forward and your heels back, back as your hands come back and your heels go forward — hit him on his quarters as his legs are gathered up for their next propulsion forward.

Never hit him on the flanks or ribs — indeed, in your first season, you may be better off just learning to slap him down the shoulder.

For the future it is also essential to be able to carry (and use) the whip in either hand. If, for instance, your horse has a tendency to hang left-handed, you must carry the whip in your left hand and be capable of slapping him down the left shoulder. However, your schoolmaster will not, hopefully, exhibit such traits and I repeat that, initially, you will be better off concerning yourself with more fundamental issues.

9

Rules, Regulations and Race Planning

For the newcomer to point-to-pointing, even looking through the racecard at a meeting may bring more questions than answers: what *is* a maiden race, for instance, and what *do* some of those abbreviations stand for? And there seems to be mention of several championships — what are they all for?

Innovations in Race Regulations

Let us first take a look at the various types of races available at a point-to-point, and the best races at which to aim a particular horse. 1992 sees some radical innovations in the permitted framework of point-to-point races.

Firstly, the number of races allowed in a programme has been increased from a limit of six to seven. If you immediately think, 'I've seen ten-race cards,' indeed, you may have, but only because some of the original races have been divided at entry. Until 1992, a seventh race in the schedule was only allowed where one of them was a cross-country members race, in addition to the ordinary hunt members race.

Other major changes are: to do away with adjacent hunts races and replace them by confined races; to change the definition of an open race simply from one open to horses from any hunt (but perhaps with some other restriction) to mean a race that is free of restriction (unless with special Jockey Club dispensation); to introduce new intermediate races; to allow open maiden races and to allow all races to be run off a 12 st. base.

Although these sound radical changes, they are nearly all examples of races that are *allowed*, but do not necessarily have to be run. Therefore, with the exception of old adjacent races becoming new confined races, it is quite possible for an unenterprising or very traditional point-to-point committee to stage exactly the same programme as it has always done. Now, indeed, instead of several types of races being compulsory per programme, the only mandatory ones are the members race and the confined race.

The confined race is in essence an extended adjacent hunts race; instead of being confined to horses from genuinely adjacent hunts, it will now be confined to horses from the fifteen hunts nearest to the host hunt (itself included).

In future a horse will be allowed to win two restricted races before being upgraded, instead of one as previously, and confined race winners will be ineligible. As before, it is designed as a stepping stone for a horse, and this has been further extended with the introduction of the new intermediate race. Restricted, maiden and confined race winners will be allowed to enter this, but open race winners or winners from under either Flat or N.H. rules will not, with the exception of winners of N.H. flat races ('bumpers'). Again, a horse will not be allowed to win more than two intermediate races.

Therefore, after a horse has won a maiden, two restricteds and two intermediates, he will only be able to run in confined, open, or members races — but many owners would be happy to think their horse could win as many as five races! It remains to be seen whether, in essence there will be much difference between a confined race and an intermediate race, other than that a confined race will allow older or failing open horses a step back down the ladder. Open races, either men's, ladies' or mixed, will continue as the 'top rung' of the point-to-point ladder. The idea behind the new specifications is to encourage greater flexibility in programmes to suit local demand and to make more competitive races. It is possible with the new framework of races allowed in 1992 that ladies races could be reduced, but I think this is unlikely because of their popularity both as a spectacle and with participants.

For any race run off a 12 st. base there are compulsory penalties for winning. From 1992 it is, therefore, going to be increasingly important to study the conditions of every race before making an entry. While this applies especially to the newcomer, I believe there will be many experienced brows considerably furrowed.

Thus the limited skeleton around which hunts (or clubs) may frame their races has been extended and as before they may make use of penalties and allowances. It should be remembered, however, that there is no handicapping in point-to-point racing and it will therefore still be quite possible for a good point-to-pointer to run up a string of successes. The new permitted framework, coupled with good race-planning by committees, should make it possible to ensure that the best horses meet in an open race, and thus bring about a better sight for spectators, at the same time give less good horses a chance in other races.

Choosing a Race

As a newcomer to the sport, you are unlikely to start on a maiden horse, that is one who has never won anything, because you have bought a schoolmaster; nevertheless, he *may* only have been placed, and so we can begin by looking at the bottom of the scale, a maiden race. There is no reason why a maiden horse should not run in other races, but usually he will run in a maiden race and, in the early part of the season in particular, there can be so many entries that the race is split into two or three divisions.

The maiden race may now be open to horses from any hunt, but, if from 'confined' hunts it should be noted that not only may the horses only come from designated hunts, but so must the riders; therefore, if a rider has his certificate from, say, the Grafton Hunt, he may only ride in 'confined' races that allow participants from that hunt.

The safety factor (the maximum number of horses the course inspector deems it safe to start on each course) for a maiden race is usually smaller than for other races. This allows for the inexperience of the horses running, but, nonetheless, I consider there is much to be said for running a horse first time out in a 'higher' race, where the number of runners is not only likely to be fewer, but also more experienced, thus reducing the risk of interference to the newcomer.

Next rung on the ladder is the restricted race, which is open to horses that have not won any race under Flat or National Hunt Rules nor any point-to-point other than a members or maiden race. After this, the new rung on the ladder is the intermediate race, followed by the confined race and finally by the open race.

With your schoolmaster point-to-pointer, the intermediate or confined race is most likely to be your target generally. Your ideal first race could be your hunt members race, but this depends on the time of year it is held. The advantages, if you can aim for it, are that usually the number of runners will be both few and experienced but not of the highest class. A disadvantage is that it is when all your chums will be there watching, so perhaps a first run out of the locality should be considered, and then be ready for a 'cut' in your home territory.

Some people will advise against running in February when fewer meetings mean greater competition, but sometimes by waiting you come against a minor setback or very firm ground and can find yourself with virtually no season left at all.

If your schoolmaster has won valuable races in the past, you may be best off running in open races or, of course, the lady rider newcomer may go straight into ladies open races. The speed is greater (horses carry less weight, for one thing) but the runners are often fairly experienced and there won't be as much lead to carry as in other races.

For most point-to-point races, the minimum weight is 12 st. 7 lb.: the exceptions are ladies opens (minimum 11 st.) and organisers may, if they choose, hold races off 12 st. so long as penalties, as stipulated by the Jockey Club, are included.

Since 1984 mares have been conceded a 5 lb. allowance in all races, and five-year-olds (the minimum age of a point-to-pointer) of either sex are allowed 7 lb. in any race. These allowances are not cumulative: in other words a five-year-old mare has a 7 lb. allowance, not 7 lb. plus 5 lb.

As far as prize money is concerned, in 1990 this was increased to a total of £250 for an open race, divided between the placed horses as decided by the hunt; and to £175 for all other races, which may include a fourth prize. (Cheques, incidentally, cannot be sent out until two weeks after the meeting in case of an objection.) In addition a perpetual challenge trophy may be presented, plus a memento of up to the value of £75 for the owner to keep; and a memento up to the value of £20 may be awarded to the winning rider.

One of the reasons point-to-pointing has remained a genuinely amateur sport is because of its modest prize-money; owners and riders are in it for love and glory but not for money.

Race Series and Championships

Various series of races may be held culminating in a final, either on a local or a national basis, and in addition most of the fourteen point-to-point administrative areas run their own area championships for leading horses and riders. Area championships usually attract a local sponsor and are generally run on a points system, horses and riders being awarded points for races run within their area but not outside it.

A typical method of scoring, as carried out by the South Midlands Area in 1990 before the new race specifications, was, for riders, four points for a win, two for a second and one for a third. For owners, it was seven, five and three points for all open race placings; six, four and two for adjacents hunts and farmers races; and four, two and one for hunt or club members races. Several areas additionally offer a novice riders championship and in the South East, at least, there is a 'wooden spoon' for the rider with most falls in the season.

The national owners and riders championships are decided on a straight wins basis; only in the event of a tie will minor places be taken into consideration. The sponsors are *The Daily Telegraph* (gentlemen riders and leading horse) and *Sporting Life* (lady riders). There are also novice and young rider awards. These trophies are presented at the annual point-to-point dinner/dance in the autumn.

There are also various series of races in which qualifying

races are held in each area culminating in a final, most of them in a hunter chase.

These include: the Land Rover Gentlemen's Open Point-to-Point Championship, staged through selected open races with its final at Towcester; RMC Group Ladies Open Point-to-Point Championship, final at Warwick; and *The Times* championship qualified through restricted open races with its final at Towcester. It is hoped to find a new sponsor to replace the successful Audi Grand Prix de Chasse adjacent hunts series with its final at the popular Cheltenham hunters evening meeting in May.

The Point-to-Point Owners Association Young Horse Awards, in which the two leading five-, six- or seven-year-olds of each Area receive an award, are presented at the Point-to-Point Owners Association Annual Lunch at Stratford and were sponsored in 1991 by *Horse and Hound*, along with the Wilkinson Sword for the leading novice rider under twenty-one, who has not ridden a winner before the start of the season. The young horse awards are based on a points system for races run anywhere in the country (not just inside a horse's own area), with open races worth ten points for a win, six for second and three for third, and eight, four and two points respectively in all other races.

Rules Relating to Entry

Entries for point-to-points close one week or more in advance, and officially are accepted in writing only. If you are late with your entry, do not expect the secretary to fit you in. He or she will probably be typing up entries all day on Sunday ready to take to the printers and copy to Weatherby's first thing on Monday morning, by which time it is certainly too late to add an entry. The printers have to have the card ready by the Saturday (preferably Friday night), and the secretary will go in during the week to proofread them all. Many hunts have a seperate entries secretary to free the overall secretary for the many administrative tasks — all of which are voluntary.

It is up to you to check the conditions of the race(s) you have entered, as you are responsible for ensuring you carry the correct weight. If you enter a race for which you are not qualified, Weatherby's will reject the entry and you will not be able to run. If you win but have not carried a necessary penalty you will be disqualified.

Each point-to-point area organisation (listed in appendix B) issues a book of schedules for every meeting within its area, and you must have one of these (or more if you live in a border area or plan to race further afield) in order to select the races and meetings at which you plan to enter. The Point-to-Point Secretaries Association (whose address is listed in appendix A), will help you with any queries.

RULES RELATING TO OWNER ELIGIBILITY For an owner to run a horse in a point-to-point, he must be a Master or member of a recognised pack of hounds in Great Britain, or else a subscriber or farmer. (This also applies to all joint owners.) He must also check that his horse is eligible for a given race, for example, his hunt membership must be to one of the hunts listed for a new confined race.

No person who has been disqualified under the Rules of Racing or point-to-pointing, or appears on the forfeit list for unpaid dues, may enter a horse.

An owner may not use an assumed name when entering or running horses. In the event of death, the deceased owner's horse may still run so long as he is described as being owned by the 'Executor(s), Administrator(s) or Personal representative(s) of ... deceased.'

The responsibilities of owners, when making entries, include agreeing to be bound by the Point-to-Point Regulations by signing the declaration included on all official entry forms.

It is up to the owner to check that his horse's passport containing vaccinations record is up to date, and to remember to bring the passport to the meeting. Failure to do so could result in a fine (£45 in 1992); he will also be duty bound to produce it within 72 hours to the Jockey Club and to sign a declaration that the horse's vaccinations are up to date before he may run.

The owner also supplies the colours to be worn by the jockey, must confirm that these are as per entry when declaring his horse, and must ensure that his jockey has them in time to weigh out.

OWNERS TO RIDE FOR, AND AVOID   Although, in the early stages, it is unlikely that a jockey will get any rides on horses not owned by himself or his family, he may, with good fortune and application, progress to the stage where 'outside' rides are offered. This may, therefore, be an appropriate moment to discuss the type of owners a jockey should ride for, and those to be avoided. The perfect owner is one who does not blame the jockey, at least in public, even if the jockey has ridden the most awful race. Split-second decisions have to be made in a race and it is all too easy for the 'grandstand jockey' with time on his side and the benefit of hindsight to be critical. The riders are, remember, amateurs — and even professionals make mistakes. Amateurs will make errors, lose races, and will all too often fall off; the worst owners are those who have never ridden themselves and do not know what it is like to face birch fences at 30 m.p.h. surrounded on all sides by other horses. However, those with the right to do so, such as former top amateurs, may take a 'new boy' on one side and quietly explain what he has done wrong, offering constructive criticism.

Heavy backers are often 'undesirable' owners; if you lose, probably the best you can hope is that the owner will simply walk away in disgust; don't expect to be offered the ride again and don't anticipate a friendly drink at his car boot. I once rode a horse on whom the owner had evidently backed heavily, who was patently 'not right'. The horse was gurgling from before half way, had his tongue hanging out and was jumping badly to the left. Eventually I did the only sensible thing and pulled him up. The owner would not speak to me after the race. The best you can do in such circumstances is 'put it down to experience.'

It is worth mentioning here that once owners start offering you 'spare' rides, it is as well to ride them at home first. Only once did I fail to do so, with desperate results, for as we approached the third, an island fence, the horse tried to run out. I attempted to keep him in, and somewhere in between a 6 ft. high wooden wing intervened. From the tremendous crack of splintering white planks and flailing hooves, I extricated myself unscathed but shaking uncontrollably. The horse, too, suffered only minor scratches, but remember you are point-to-pointing for fun, so do and try and find out in advance about 'spare' rides.

RULES RELATING TO RIDER ELIGIBILITY   Riders, too, have to be eligible to point-to-point, and there are a number of further point-to-point rules and regulations for the newcomer to make careful note of.

Firstly, the minimum age for a rider of either sex is sixteen, and there is no upper age limit; (under N.H. rules, riders have to pass a medical if they wish to continue riding after the age of 35). In 1991, two boy riders aged sixteen, Guy Lewis and Trevor Marks, shared the leading male novice prize.

Secondly, every point-to-point rider must hold a current Riders' Qualification Certificate and must have paid the required fee for the point-to-point riders' personal accident scheme. The certificate must be signed by a hunt secretary who declares in what respect the rider is qualified. (Rider qualifications are the same as for owners, except that serving members of H.M. Forces, and members of a military service, club or unit, may ride in races confined to them without being otherwise qualified.)

You must take your rider's certificate with you every time you plan to ride in a race, and it would be wise to have it with you even when without a booked ride in case you get offered one at the last minute. Failure to produce your certificate when the horse is declared will result in an automatic fine which, for 1992, is £30. In such cases, you will also be required to sign a declaration that you do hold the certificate, and you will have to forward it to the Jockey Club Registry Office for inspection within 72 hours, so it is much better to keep your certificate in a safe place that will ensure its arrival at the course. It is worth remembering, also, that although the rider does not declare a horse, unless he is also the owner or has a written authority to act, it is at declaration, not at weighing out, that the certificate is needed.

Thirdly, you must also make certain that you are eligible to ride in the race for which you are declared. An open race should pose no problem, but in a confined race you, as well as the horse, must hold your certificate from one of the eligible hunts (not necessarily the same one as the horse) and, for a farmers, club, or military race, you as well as the owner must fulfill the qualification obligations.

Restrictions on former professional riders in point-to-points have eased in recent years. At one time, if a person had been in hunt service, say, for just a few months of his life, that barred him forever from point-to-pointing. Equally, a failed professional jockey, however brief his career, was banned from the amateur game for life. It is, of course, quite right that professionals should be barred from an amateur sport, but the rules for ex-professionals have been eased. A professional jockey of more than one year's standing is still ineligible to point-to-point, but an apprentice jockey (from the flat) or a conditional jockey (under N.H. rules) or a N.H. jockey whose licence was issued prior to July 1979 (in the 1992 point-to-point season) may ride, provided that the licence was surrendered within 30 months of its issue.

However, anyone whose principle paid occupation at any time in the last year has been to ride or groom for a licenced trainer or permit holder (even if the permit is held by a family member) is banned, as is anyone who has been a paid huntsman, kennel huntsman or whipper-in within the last year.

If an amateur rider under Rules is either disqualified or suspended, that person may not ride in a point-to-point during the period of disqualification or suspension.

10

The Racecard and Bookmakers

The Racecard

The newcomer to point-to-pointing may initially find that the racecard takes a bit of understanding. Apart from a number of advertisements, which volunteers will have gleaned to help pay for the printing, it will list the races in order, giving both the time of the race, and the time by which declarations must be made (three-quarters of an hour in advance), as well as the name of the race, including its sponsor.

It will give the race conditions, but not necessarily the prize money, and will probably list the entries in alphabetical order. Apart from the horse's name it will also give breeding, age, owner and rider. It will probably use abbreviations for the horse's colour and sex, hence b.g. stands for bay gelding, ch.m. for chestnut mare and so on. Likewise, the hunt with which the horse is qualified may be abbreviated, hence VAH stands for Vale of Aylesbury Hunt and so on. Also listed will be the colours to be worn by the jockey, which is of particular use to spectators.

The card may also show the previous form of each entry; apart from the obvious 1, 2, 3 for first, second, third, it may include b.d. for brought down; u for unseated rider; f for fell; s for slipped up; blkd for baulked; p for pulled up; r for refused; ref or tnp for refused to start or took no part.

Additionally, many racecards today incorporate a form guide, designed to help the punter, and this will include a rating — the higher the figure, the better the chances of the horse on form, with 000 or NR (not rated) meaning the horse appears to have no chance on previous known form.

Bookmakers and Betting

Hand-in-hand with horseracing goes betting, and point-to-pointing is no exception. All point-to-points have bookmakers, who pay the host hunt a set fee for their pitches, after which all profits belong to them.

Many meetings also have a totalisator; this used to be the Official Horserace Totalisator but they have become far more select about the meetings they attend in recent years and only a few remain. Instead, many hunts run their own tote, and this has become an additional source of revenue. The totalisator is an official registry of money staked on horses in a race; the amount of dividend is worked out mathematically, the sum pooled being divided among backers of the winner in proportion to their stakes. The tote is housed in a long tent with a line of grilled windows on one side with signs saying £5 or £1; here people queue up to place their bets. The other side has a similar line of windows for paying out winnings. Inside the tent, the officials work out the winning dividend the moment the winner passes the post and it is announced shortly after the 'winner weighed in' call is announced.

Bookmakers work out their own odds, but again these will go with the public's trend, and are therefore likely to be similar to the tote. The more money punters place on one horse, the shorter that horse's odds will be.

The bookmaker has a blackboard bearing his name at the top, a clerk with a ledger in which every bet is noted, and a large, bulky satchel in which he stores his cash. He chalks up the names of the declared runners for the next race on the blackboard. On the left hand side beside each name he will write the odds. The figure 4 besides a horse's name indicates the bookmaker considers his odds of winning the race to be four to one against; that is, if the punter bets £1 and the horse wins, he will receive his £1 stake plus £4 in winnings (less betting tax deducted by the bookmaker and forwarded to H.M. Customs and Excise). When placing a bet, the punter receives a numbered ticket from the bookmaker, whose assistant makes a note of the transaction in his ledger.

The bookie calls out the odds, urging punters to bet with him. He has an assistant who keeps his eyes peeled to see what odds other bookies are offering. If the price of a horse comes tumbling down, it is part of the punter's fun to see if he can still find a bookie quoting that horse at longer odds before they, too, shorten. This will happen in moments, because bookies have a sign language known as tic tac; the tic tac men signal to their bookmaker what odds their rivals are offering, their gesticulations being the equivalent of double dutch to the layman.

Some betting terms include slang for different amounts of money; a 'pony' is £25; a 'century' £100; a 'monkey' is £500 and a 'grand' is £1,000. An each way bet is a bet of an equal amount of money for both win and place on the same horse. A place normally covers the first three home in fields of eight of more, but just beware in a point-to-point because, even with many runners, a bookie will often pay place money on the first two only. If you have a place bet only and the horse wins, you still receive only place money, usually one fifth of the odds of a win bet.

When a bookmaker shouts 'six to four the field', he means this is the shortest price, and all the other runners are the same odds or longer. If he shouts 'six to one bar one', he means that all except one horse (the favourite) are at these or longer odds. Odds-on means that a punter has to place a stake greater than the amount he will win so that, supposing a horse is two to one on (usually written 1–2), for every £2 that the punter stakes, he will only receive £1 in winnings, (although he will, of course, also get his stake money back).

Bookmakers, including those at point-to-points, all belong to the Bookmakers Association (B.M.A.), and their trade is controlled by the Tattersalls Committee. Gone are the days when a bookmaker might 'welsh', that is, disappear quickly when he realised he owed a lot of winnings. If a bookie stands to lose a lot of money as a result of a punter placing a particularly large bet with him, he may 'lay it off' with other bookmakers; that is, the bet is shared between a number of colleagues, although the punter deals only with the one with which he laid the bet. This practice is also known as 'hedging' a bet.

The bookies' row makes a colourful scene and is very much a part of the traditional British atmosphere, even though for years there have been detractors who want them banned in favour of a Tote monopoly in order that the profits may be ploughed back into the sport that gives them their living, racing.

Riders should note that, under the Rules of Racing, jockeys are not allowed to bet, for the very good reason that financial involvement might, shall we say, cloud their judgement. However, friends and relatives enjoy the bookmaking scene, and tend to show touching loyalty in supporting 'their' horse with fivers — a gesture which heightens either their euphoria or their criticism of your riding, depending upon the result!

11

Clothing, Tack and Supplementary Equipment

The Jockey's Clothing

One of the proudest moments for a new owner is seeing his or her colours worn for the first time, and for the owner/rider when they wear them.

Colours do not have to be registered for point-to-pointing but they do for hunter chasing, so it is as well to do so; otherwise should you find yourself aiming for a hunter chase you may find your point-to-point colours unavailable for registration.

You are best advised to have woollen colours rather than silks unless you are very tight for weight, as it can be very cold in the early spring. The cap cover, however, will be silk or nylon.

The jersey and cap are all the owner has to provide for the jockey's wear, and the jockey has to have these with him at the scales.

Regarding the rest of the jockey's gear; the wearing of a body protector is now compulsory. This has taken over from the back pad and, as the name implies, offers better overall protection. The patterns approved by the Jockey Club are (for 1992) *Air-O-Wear*, *Besafe*, *Chase Designs*, *How's Racesafe*, *Porta*, *Ransome* and *Robin*. For comfort, it is advisable to wear a tee shirt or vest under the body protector.

The skull cap must not only be one bearing the Kite Mark approved to British Standard BS4472, but must also be correctly fitted, and the chin strap must be fastened at all times when the rider is mounted. The stewards have the authority, which they exercise from time to time, to check the fitting. Remember, the drawstrings inside must be fastened tightly enough to allow a cushion of air between string and cap. The harness must be adjusted to fit the individual rider and don't forget that, if you have a heavy fall, it may be necessary to discard your helmet, even if external damage is not apparent. This is not an occasion for penny pinching.

When fitting the cap cover, tuck the back a little way under the helmet, thread the tie strings through the ear harness to prevent the cover from falling off (or use a large elastic band), and tie it securely in front, preferably enlisting someone else to hold the first knot tight with a finger while the second knot is tied. Then tie a bow and tuck the ends under the part that circles the cap. If the ends are very long, consider cutting them: you do not want loose ends flapping in front of your eyes in a race.

It is advisable to have a pair of goggles, and to practise wearing them at home. They should be placed above the peak of the cap, and only pulled down just before the start of the race, or they may steam up. Lady riders should tuck long hair into a net or tie it back in a pony tail.

Around the neck you should tie a stock, not so tight that you cannot breathe, but tight enough to offer protection in the event of a fall. I don't advise using a pin, just knot it and tuck the tails under your jumper.

Thin gloves are much to be recommended, of the sort that will grip well, such as fishnet or with rubber pimples (like rubber reins). Gloves are useful to prevent the reins slipping when a horse sweats a lot or if it is raining, and especially in holding a puller. If the colours provided are rather large, it is helpful to put elastic bands round the cuffs to keep them clear of your hands.

As far as breeches are concerned, I prefer cotton to nylon, since the former are less slippery. When buying racing breeches, remember to allow enough room for the body protector. Many riders, including men, wear ladies tights underneath their breeches, unless the weather is very hot.

Because you should be riding with your feet 'right home' in

the stirrups, bringing the stirrup leathers right up against your shins, it is also a good idea to wear shin guards under your boots, especially as racing boots are very thin. Incidentally, if weight is no problem, there is nothing wrong with wearing your leather hunting boots to race in, and they offer good protection. Otherwise, acquire yourself some proper racing boots; you will probably become quite sentimentally attached to them, and keep them long after you have 'hung up your boots'.

Spurs are only occasionally worn racing. If you have a horse who needs them, note that you are not permitted to wear spurs which are sharp, angled, or fitted with rowels, and they may be inspected when you weigh out.

Also, if you need to wear either spectacles or contact lenses, bear in mind that, although not forbidden, the Jockey Club strongly recommend against the wearing of spectacles in races, and recommend that contact lenses should be of the soft or perma type. They further recommend that a metal disc inscribed 'wearer using contact lenses' should be worn when racing, and such discs are available from the licensing department of the Jockey Club.

Regarding the whip, we have already looked at the permitted sizes, and it should be easy to get one from a good saddler. Mark the inside of the flaps with your name, in case you drop it; also, fasten an elastic band round it just below where you will be holding it, to prevent it slipping right through your hand.

Last but not least of the rider's requirements is to remember to take your rider's certificate with you to every meeting.

Tack

The bridle is the owner's responsibility, but the saddle is the rider's, including girth, stirrup leathers and irons, surcingle and breastplate or girth, and it is the rider's responsibility to see that the saddle is in fit condition.

Although it is officially the owner's responsibility to ensure that the horse is properly saddled, there is no stipulation as to who should supply the weight cloth and weights. However, since it is the rider who has to weigh out correctly, it is best if he assumes responsibility for these items. You are almost certain to need a weight cloth, if only because scales can vary from course to course. It fits under the saddle, like a saddle cloth. Lead weights, available in 1 lb. and ½ lb. slabs to fit the pockets of the weight cloth, are available from good saddlers. It is best to place most of the weight in the forward compartments of the cloth, which itself should be placed well forward on the horse. In this way, most of the burden will fall on the horse's shoulders, and will not be flapping about each side of his loins. It is also sensible to have a practise weigh at home, having established the exact weight the horse is due to carry, and then allow a few pounds either way, as scales at point-to-points can vary in accuracy (or yours at home may be wrong).

With the exception of lady riders, who could ride between 10 st. 7 lbs. on a five-year-old in a ladies race and 13 st. on a horse with a 7 lb. penalty in an adjacent race, there is not normally a wide weight range in point-to-points. In most cases, therefore, a rider should be able to choose one saddle to suit all needs. Even if weight is no problem to you, and you are only planning a 'bump round in the hunt race', do not use a hunting saddle; you will be much better off in a racing saddle, even if you have to borrow one.

Mine was a 21 lb. weighted racing saddle, but even so I had to carry a weight cloth, and two in 12 st. 7 lb. races. If you can have a saddle of between about 7 and 12 lb. without either having to waste too hard or carry too much lead, that is ideal. However, if weight is a problem, don't worry too much about using a tiny 2 lb. saddle. It might feel like sitting on a knife edge as you walk round the paddock, but once you are cantering to the start, or galloping in a race, your seat will be out of the saddle anyway and you simply won't notice it.

You are unlikely to need a numnah or saddle cloth since the number cloth issued at the scales and included in the weighing out will act as the latter. You may, however, use a dampened chamois leather next to the horse's skin, either as a wither pad or saddle cloth, since this will act as an extra safeguard against the saddle slipping. Non-slip, high density foam is also good for this.

Use narrow, unbreakable stirrup leathers, and racing irons of a correct size for your foot. Elasticated or webbing racing girths, which always come in pairs, are best.

The bridle, provided by the owner should be the smartest available, and it is nice if it has a rolled and stitched noseband and stitched browband, or a coloured 'dragonsteeth' browband to match the owner's racing colours. The bit should be a jointed D-ring snaffle; only very occasionally should a different type of bit be needed. The reins must be rubber covered for extra grip, (some people will use plaited reins, but I believe rubber reins are the only type to use, and plain leather reins should *never* be used). The reins should be stitched or fastened by buckle. They should also be slightly narrower than hunting reins and should be long enough to allow the rider to 'give' but not so long that they may loop around the rider's foot. Buckled reins should be knotted at the end as a safeguard against the buckle breaking or becoming unfastened.

An Irish martingale (sometimes known as rings) should be used, to keep the reins together. Again, only in very exceptional circumstances should a running martingale be used; I have seen the use of one pull a horse down at a fence when without it he may have been able to find a 'fifth' leg.

It is imperative to have either a breastplate or breastgirth, as well as a surcingle. You may think your horse will never have his saddle slip, but towards the end of three miles at racing pace he could have shed several pounds, and so these extra safety precautions are essential. The breastplate or girth has to be declared to the clerk of the scales upon weighing out, and is included in the rider's overall weight, as is the surcingle.

If your horse wears blinkers, these will have been declared to the declarations clerk; again, the rider must have them when weighing out, as they are included.

It will also be necessary to provide a lead rein and coupling for the handler who leads the horse round the paddock and it is preferable if this is made of white webbing, which can be cleaned with shoe whitener.

Whether you run your horse in boots or bandages, or nothing at all, depends partly on individual choice and partly on past record. Bandages must only be applied by someone who really

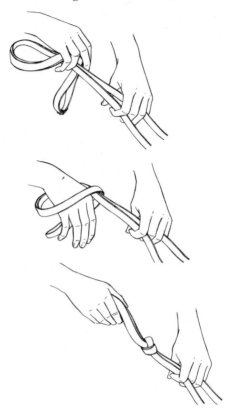

Knotting the reins

knows what they are doing, or more harm than good may result. The horse's legs will swell in the heat caused by his exertions, and if the bandages are too tight, permanent damage to the tendons – the very things you are trying to protect – may be caused. Equally, if they are too loose, they may fall down and cause the horse to trip. Gamgee should be wrapped around the legs under bandages, to help absorb the expansions and contractions.

Out hunting, boots can cause more harm than good if a bit of grit or mud gets inside and rubs the leg for several hours, but this is less likely during the few minutes of a race, and boots do offer good protection against birch marks or from being struck into. The velcro fastenings of today's boots makes them very easy to put on, but the same points as for bandaging apply and care must be taken.

Supplementary Equipment

It is wise to have a suitcase in which you carry the basic requirements for the care and needs of the horse, and to keep it in a state of readiness from week to week.

In this you will need a sweatsheet, essential to place over your horse immediately after he is unsaddled after his race. You should also have a paddock sheet and surcingle, and it is nice if you can have one which picks up your colours, the main colour for the rug and a minor one for its border piping. It is only in very warm weather that you will not need to parade your horse in this sheet, and when it is cold, instead of stripping it right off as soon as the horse is mounted, the jockey should fold it back and sit on it until the moment the handler lets go of the horse, when he will also take the sheet. As with an athlete, it is important to keep your horse's muscles warm before the race.

Essential first aid equipment includes a poultice such as Animalintex and a bandage with which to fasten it; antiseptic spray or cream and wound powder, and scissors. Other items to remember are a bucket and a large container of water. If your horse gives himself speedy cuts, where the shoe of one hind leg catches the inside of the other hind leg just below the hock (and above a boot), you should pack some sticky tape to apply as protection when you prepare him.

Grooming kit must also be packed. Although the main grooming will be done at home, put in a soft brush and a cloth for the final polish. You will also need a sponge for wiping the horse's eyes and mouth before the race and for washing him off afterwards; and a sweat scraper following that.

If your horse has to run in a tongue strap (a gadget occasionally used if a horse is inclined to swallow his tongue) keep this packed in the case. Also note that, on the day, its fitting has to be inspected by the course vet, and it is up to you to notify him.

A haynet should be included for the return journey only. Remember to tie up your horse to breakable string in the lorry or trailer and, if he is allergic to straw, make sure there is none on the floor of the vehicle.

Finally, but most importantly, keep the horse's passport permanently packed.

12

The Race

At last the day dawns for your first ride in a point-to-point; your horse fit, yourself fit enough to do him justice – and you draw back the curtains on to an eerie, silent, white world, blanketed by snow. How often the weather intervenes in early February...

There is nothing for it but to wait another week, and those around you must put up with your nerves for a bit longer. It is at a time like this that you convince yourself that you were *bound* to have won! However, when it does come to the actual day, your dreams of winning soon become fervent hopes simply for a good ride round...

Preparation

PRE-RACE HOMEWORK   Do some homework before the race. Know and recognise the riders' colours of those horses most likely to be in the shake-up and plan to stay within reach of them. (However, don't ignore the prospects of 'unknown quantities'. It is all too easy, having tracked a 'good thing', to be beaten by an unconsidered rival.) Equally important, know the colours of those with a bad jumping record or whose rider has a reputation for weaving around – and make sure you don't become one yourself. It is *imperative* to keep a straight line when racing, especially on the approach to a fence, for the safety of all concerned.

Also in your homework, watch how races are run and won on different courses; whether the winner has usually been leading for a long way or whether he usually comes from behind; whether the run-in is a long or short one, uphill or downhill. See which fences seem to be causing most trouble, and observe how the experienced riders put their racecraft to good use.

THE HORSE Have everything prepared and packed the night before. Give your horse only a little hay and if he has cleared up his hard feed, try giving him a little more. Give only a small feed in the morning, and no hay. Have him plaited unless this makes him break out into a sweat or tremble with anticipation. Plaits not only look smart, they will prevent you from getting bits of mane tangled up in your fingers.

Leave in good time, always allow 'breakdown' time, and reach the course with time for your horse to settle and for you to walk the course. On arrival, lead the horse round for a while to loosen him up after the journey (don't let him nibble grass), then re-load him while you walk the course.

WALKING THE COURSE If you are unsure how long this will take, you should declare first, unless you don't intend to make a decision about running until you have seen the state of the ground. You may have walked the course during the week, but walk it again on the day, something you must do throughout your career. David Tatlow, four times champion point-to-point jockey in the 1960s and now a top show rider, names walking the course, preferably twice, as one of his golden rules. In my own case, the luckiest win I ever had was on an Easter Monday when, in a three-horse race, both my rivals went the wrong side of a marker, a flag which had not been put in place earlier in the week...

As you walk the course make a note of the bends, of any poached or rough ground, the stiffness of the fences, and, of course, the positioning of the markers; red flags to be passed on your right, white on your left. Also make a note of the siting of a fence in relation to the line of the ropes, as it may mean 'coming off the ropes' to get a straight line to the fence. Watch out for any adverse cambers, and make a mental note to have your horse well held together at such places. The majority of point-to-point courses are set on ordinary farmland and although clerks of courses will do their utmost to have courses harrowed and in good shape, nothing can be done about natural gradients.

Where there are hilly courses, watch out not only for drop fences but also fences where you land on rising ground. This can catch you out and prop you over your horse's head if you are not ready for it. Likewise, with a drop fence, be prepared to lean back from the waist, slip your reins and have your lower legs well forward, as practised in training.

When you are on your feet the fences may look huge and fearsome, but once you are mounted and you show your horse the first fence you will be looking down on it, and suddenly it will not seem so big.

DECLARING AND PERSONAL PREPARATION On your return, go to the secretary's tent to declare, taking both your rider's certificate and horse's passport with you. Remember to declare blinkers if your horse is to wear them.

Change in good time, but not so early that time hangs — there is nothing worse for nerves than waiting. You have to weigh out at least a quarter of an hour before your race but, in practice, you will weigh out sooner than this (unless you have ridden in the previous race.) Dress tidily and make sure you tuck your sweater in; riding with a sweater outside the breeches is the biggest dead give-away of a novice newcomer.

You would be unwise to eat or drink before a race, and you are unlikely to want to. Try and have a reasonable breakfast at home, and make sure someone saves you some food for after your race. Some changing tents provide sandwiches and squash. A nip of 'Dutch courage', so long as it is no more than a nip, may be all right, but if ever you reach the stage of needing more, it is time to hang up your boots.

WEIGHING OUT AND SADDLING UP When you weigh out, you do so without your skull cap and whip, although you should have both with you for inspection, and you will be allowed an extra pound for the back protector which is now mandatory. The clerk of the scales or his assistant will provide

Weighing out

you with the correct number cloth for your horse and this is included in your weight. The horse must be saddled so that the number is clearly visible to spectators. You must have your cap cover with you, as the clerk of the scales will also check that you are wearing the correct colours. There is no fine for wrong colours in a point-to-point, but if they are different from those printed on the racecard, an announcement will be made and a notice on the number board will be posted telling the public the colours that are being carried.

Have someone experienced saddle up for you, who will also assist you in the paddock. You don't have to be there to saddle unless you particularly want to be. If you decide to do it yourself, place the wither pad on first, and have somebody each side of the horse to hold such things in place and keep them equal on both sides. The horse's handler should stand in front of the horse, facing him, with a hand on each rein just behind the bit. Put the number cloth in place last thing before the saddle, making sure that the number shows clearly.

Remember to have the saddle well forward; don't forget to put on the weight cloth (mine was left off once; on unsaddling I braced myself for the usual heavy weight only to nearly fall backwards as it was so light: the ensuing disqualification was inevitable.) Don't tighten the girths so much that they pinch the horse or so he can hardly breath, just have them tight enough to hold everything in place. The girths should be checked again in the paddock, as well as down at the start. Have the breastplate or girth adjusted so that there is about a hand's width of freedom between it and the horse's chest. Cross the irons over the saddle, and knot the end of the reins either now or when you are mounted.

FINAL ARRANGEMENTS, MOUNTING AND GOING TO POST

Put on the paddock sheet, secure it with a surcingle, and send the horse straight into the paddock. The regulations state that the horse should be there in 'reasonable time', which is generally interpreted as having time to walk a few circuits before being mounted, and again with the rider.

When the horse goes into the parade ring, you return to the changing tent, sort out your hat, gloves and whip, chat with the other riders, gleaning what information you can about their rides, and wait for the call to the paddock.

David Tatlow describes the atmosphere in the changing room as the thing he still misses most about race-riding:

It is the most wonderful place on a racecourse, and you must always remember that 90 per cent in that tent are either as nervous as you or are very willing to help you before, during and after the race.

Very few riders are anything other than totally considerate to beginners, so don't be in any way ashamed of telling them all it is your first race; you will get more help and kindness if they know it.

In the paddock, join your owner if that is not yourself, and either your helper, wife, girlfriend, father — whoever it is whose moral support you most want (but no children) — and for a moment or two, discuss plans for the umpteenth time.

Race-riding plans should always be flexible so that the circumstances of the actual race can be taken into consideration as they occur.

When the bell goes and the paddock steward calls 'Jockeys get mounted please', the horses' heads are turned inwards and you walk towards your horse, doing up your chin strap as you go. Girths are checked, within moments you are lightly legged up into the saddle — and, as if by magic, those butterflies churning inside your stomach fly away. The feel of a fit, eager horse beneath you is a marvellous sensation, and as the huntsman signals a short toot on his horn you eagerly follow him down to the start.

Canter down at a nice steady pace. There is nothing more nerve-shattering than being run away with down to the start. It happened to me the only time I ever rode at Badbury Rings: feeling extra well, old Tarka Otter gradually gained momentum and lengthened his stride down that hill towards the start and before I knew it he was 'carting' me, only to stop dead when he reached the other runners, dropping me off like a sack of potatoes. No wonder the starter enquired, 'Has she ever ridden before?'

If you know your horse pulls hard, don't let him out of a hack canter down to the start; this may necessitate forcing him to canter with his head tucked to one side. Try to go alone so that he does not 'race' other horses as they overtake him, and whatever happens, don't try and shorten the reins to gain a firmer hold of him, because in the instant that manoeuvre takes he will be gone. Permission may be sought from the stewards to go down early, which is well worthwhile.

The Start

Once you are at the start you are under the control of the starter and, if you disobey him or are rude, he may report you to the stewards of the meeting. Listen to what the starter may say; he will inform you whether he wants a standing start or whether he allows you to walk in; he may have important information regarding a fence or a bend; or if a horse is being

Going to post: *a) setting off correctly*

b) setting off incorrectly

unruly, he may order that he be held behind the others. (If you need your horse held at the start, seek the starter's permission, which will be given subject to the horse being held at a standstill behind the other runners, so that you cannot gain an advantage.)

The starter is not the only official with a flag; his flagman, or assistant, has one, too, and he will place himself about one hundred yards down the course, before the first fence. His job is to confirm the start by dropping his flag once the starter has done so, but if there is a false start — that is, a number of horses start running before the starter's flag is dropped — the flagman will keep his flag raised and will stay on the course himself. Therefore, if you see him with his flag still raised you must pull up and return to the start. Thankfully, false starts are not a common occurrence.

The importance of a good start is sometimes overlooked. Things happen quickly in a race, and to have got off to a good start is vitally important, a fact confirmed by David Tatlow who says, 'I was always told of the importance of the start, and after twenty years of race-riding I can totally confirm that is correct.'

He also advocates the newcomer arranging for a 'wise old head' to go down to the start to talk to you, calm any pre-race nerves and to mention to the starter that you are a new boy (or girl):

I found starters to be the kindest and most considerate of people. A good start makes your first race so much easier than a bad one. I have never believed in giving ground away at the start. I could never see the sense in it unless you have a very highly strung horse who must be dropped out at the beginning.

Having reached the start, walk up to the first fence, show it to your horse, pat his neck, turn and hack quietly back to the start where the assistant starter will check your girths and the starter will go through the roll-call.

From this moment on, be watching the starter with one eye and your fellow riders with the other, walking in a fairly tight circle ready to line up in a good place the moment the starter calls you in. One rider may have warned that his horse jumps to the right; this may be so and is helpful, but equally, on a right-handed course, it may be a bit of gamesmanship from the rider wanting to bag the inside! Even before the starter calls you to line up, sharp riders will be jockeying for position, and the inside berths will be filled quickly by experienced riders. There can be occasions when it is better not to be hugging the inside, certainly on your first ride, or if riding a faint-hearted horse who will be better off seeing more daylight. It is important anyway that your horse gets a good sight of the first fence. The late Sue Aston had no peer at the art of riding glued to the inside, and many races can be won by going the shortest way but if attempting to do so is going to lead to scrimmaging in the early stages of a race, it is better to swallow your pride and go a bit wide.

At the start, also watch out for the old hand who will try and jump the gun, a practice that can intimidate an inexperienced starter who is, after all, simply an unpaid volunteer of the hunt. I remember one rider in particular who would start her horse and, once she had gone several lengths, the starter sometimes then rather feebly dropped his flag. Only once was I left waiting in vain for what should have been the assistant starter's inevitable recall flag...

When the starter raises his flag, you are then 'under starter's orders' and you must form a line, catch hold of your horse's head, and watch the starter acutely, having first pulled down your goggles. These protect your eyes from flying mud or dust, but if you pull them down too long before the start they will steam up. Hold your reins in a single bridge which ensures an even pressure (and hold the reins inside your little finger), and be ready to go! A bad start may never be recovered from, so don't listen to those who say it doesn't matter when there are three miles to go.

If you do get a bad start, don't try and make up the ground in a rush. It is better to get a good start and then settle back into your desired position, so never go to sleep at the start. If your horse whips round or, worse, 'plants' himself when you are already under starter's orders, call out, 'Wait, sir; no, sir.' The starter should do all he can to ensure everyone gets a good, clean, fair break.

The Early Stages

As part of your pre-race mental homework, divide the race into three parts. Most circuits are a little under one and a half miles, completed twice with one to three fences jumped three times, but remember when 'sectioning' a course in your mind that a course like Larkhill, for instance, is very long and Umberleigh in Devon is so short that there is special Jockey Club dispensation for the circuit to be completed almost three times.

The first mile or so will be simply about surviving and remaining on your horse's back, preferably within the leading quarter of runners (tactics will come later in your career). If you are able to think at all at this stage you have probably been well coached, but it is more likely that the first few fences will flash by so quickly that a new rider will wonder what on earth happened to them! However the good schoolmaster knows what he is doing, will quicken into his fences, and know when to take off.

You are also quite likely to have forgotten to breathe! Many sportsmen realise the importance of learning to breath properly and racing should be no exception, otherwise you may end the race not only breathless but also with a searing pain through your chest, especially if there is also a biting east wind. So at least make a point of breathing over each fence and you won't get so blown.

There is a lot of noise in a race, both from the sound of hooves, of birch crackling as the fences are jumped, and from the cheering crowds, but you will probably be so absorbed in the race itself that you will take no notice of this.

Keep still on your horse, have a nice even length of rein with a contact on the mouth that is just firm enough, with your hands low and neat near the withers, preferably just each side of the neck; have your seat raised a few inches out of the saddle (not high like Lester Piggott, but not bumping around in the saddle); lean forward from the waist so that you are looking ahead through your horse's ears, but straighten up a little as you come into a fence; have your elbows in but slightly bent to allow some give and take; don't pull on your horse's mouth or 'hail a cab' (take one hand off the reins and hold it high in the air for balance as you jump); keep your feet right home in the stirrups; get your lower legs forwards over the fences; be prepared to slip the reins if you need to give your horse his head more, and collect him smoothly as you land. Squeeze with your legs in rhythm with the horse for a few strides going into a fence, and give him that little bit of extra 'offing' into the open ditch (a fence horses normally jump well); Above all, keep him straight.

It is early in a race, when the runners are bunched, that you are most likely to be blinded at a fence. Don't panic; your experienced horse will have a much better idea than you about what to do, and will take off at the right moment. The danger is if one of the horses ahead of you falls, but this is where your policy of following 'safe' runners should pay off. If one does fall, your horse will do all he can to avoid him, but be ready for his swerving action.

Notwithstanding this, you must *try* and avoid unsighting your horse through getting *too* close to the horse in front of you. You may be able to pull out a bit, but only if you have glanced over your shoulder to ensure you won't in turn be impeding somebody else. The worst point-to-point fall I had occurred when a rider shot from last to first place before the first fence, crossing directly in front of my horse a stride before take off. My horse went into an undeserved cartwheel and left me with a whip-lashed neck and minus a few teeth.

Some fences, perhaps just one of the eighteen, your horse will meet wrong. There is no time to take drastic measures to put him right as there may be in other sports; to 'hook back' like a showjumper would be a sure way of losing a race, and would court trouble from a following horse running into your heels, and anyway, it is simply not part of the make up of a racehorse's mentality. Instead, it is down to a split-second decision: you may steady him up a bit to try and help him put himself right; or you may kick him and slap him down the shoulder to ask him for a 'long one'; or, probably best for the novice rider, sit tight, brace yourself, and let him 'fiddle' it.

Horses seldom win from in front over three miles unless exceptionally good, but if you have a confirmed front runner

Standing off

Fiddling

who revels in blazing a trail, he may prove disappointing if you hold him back. The most exhilarating jumper I ever rode was called Comci Comca but when, just once, it was tried 'holding him up' to help him stay the distance, he just didn't want to know, sulked, and ran abysmally.

The Middle Stages

Once the first mile or so has been completed, the race will be beginning to take shape, and with any luck you will still be up in the thick of it. The middle stages are where the beginner may start either using his horse too much or 'losing his pitch'. The novice rider, says David Tatlow, is neither entitled to think he has gone so fast that the others can't keep up with him, nor that they have gone too fast and will come back to him. 'Let the experienced riders be the judge of pace and your guide,' he says.

If your horse is beginning to drop back, try giving him a couple of 'reminders'; a slap or two down the shoulder perhaps, because he may simply be 'having you on'. Do this *before* you have got out of touch and, with luck, he will take hold of the bit and run on again. If he gets very tired, however, pull him up rather than risk a fall. In fact, knowing when to pull up is the next of David Tatlow's golden rules:

When it enters your head that you may need to pull up, do it there and then; don't say to yourself 'I will jump two more and pull up', because those are the two that are likely to give you your fall. Always remember you are better off to pull up one fence too soon rather than too late.

The Final Stages

Let us assume you are still in a nice position. By this time most races have sorted themselves out, leaving four or five horses with a chance so, from that point of view, it is becoming easier because there are fewer horses around. Often at this stage, the pace will be 'hotting up' and even if it is not quickening on the flat, it is in the last mile of the race that you notice the quickening of the horses jumping, probably because

Dealing with a mistake
Correct sequence: a) On realising that the horse is going to hit a fence, the jockey should sit up, straighten his back, brace his lower legs and allow the horse a good length of rein

b) This posture should be maintained, as far as possible, in flight

c) On landing, the jockey must sit back and allow the horse all the rein he needs to rebalance himself

they have warmed up, but also because this is where the good jumpers are trying to gain advantage in the air.

This is where the 'half-length' rule is most likely to come into play. It is especially important when you are inexperienced to jump either upsides another horse or one length behind. The trap of being 'half-lengthed' is a very real one and can lure you into a fall, as previously mentioned. Once, before women could ride in anything other than ladies races, my sister Patsy Smiles and I found ourselves compelled to contest the same race, (at Aldington) and it resulted in a tremendous duel. Gradually, the two stable companions, Aultroy and Rough Scot, drew away from the rest and, approaching the slightly downhill third last fence, I remember thinking, 'Crikey, she can't go that fast into it!' However, to have been 'half-lengthed' at this speed would have been fatal, so I kept with her and over we both flew. The only pity was that either horse (or rider) had to be the loser...

At this stage of the race, don't try and make up ground when going up hill, or round the outside of a bend, and don't try and make up ground too quickly; this could lead to a mistake at a fence, possibiy unseating you. Keep it gradual:

Dealing with a mistake
Incorrect sequence: a) Although the jockey's body is somewhat back, failure to 'give' rein means that his spin is curled forward rather than being properly braced

b) This leads to security of posture being lost when the horse hits the fence

c) An insecure seat cannot counteract the twin effects of deceleration and being pulled forward by too short reins

there is plenty of time before the winning post is reached. The same applies after a bad mistake; this will 'knock the stuffing' out of your horse and you must give him time to recover and get back into his stride, even if the mistake occurs at the last fence.

Watch out for loose horses; they seldom fall but will usually run out and, if you come between them and their exit, they may carry you out with them, a disaster that can happen very quickly. If necessary, wave your whip at a loose horse to head him off.

You may or may not turn out to be a 'natural' at judging pace, but if you are still well in contention with a couple of fences to go in your first race, your adrenalin will be flowing, and you will experience that desire to get 'first run' — that will to win which is the natural competitor's instinct.

Ideally, you want to begin your forward move about two fences from home, and take the lead as you approach the last (if you have been able to slip through on the inside, you will indeed be a jockey as well as a horseman; equally, if your horse is beaten, concede the inside to a challenger coming through). However, still keep as quiet as you can, even if all those around you seem to be kicking for dear life. Don't start getting too excited, don't start bumping around in the saddle with loose reins flapping, and don't make the mistake of riding into the last fence 'as if it isn't there' or your poor horse may respond accordingly and fail to rise. If you can 'see' a stride you may 'ask' for a big leap and this may win the race, but otherwise it is better to sit still and fiddle it, at least until you are much more experienced. On landing, don't bustle your horse, pick him up, balance him, and then ride. Also, don't start flailing your whip.

David Tatlow is adamant:

If you have been lucky in your guidance before your first race your mentor will have said whatever you do, don't think of picking up your stick in a finish. Very few amateurs ever learn to use a stick in a finish correctly. I have seen so many races lost by do-lallies waving sticks around. It is important when you consider riding a finish that the first place a horse gets tired is his neck, therefore it is very important that you keep hold of his head, so he has something to lean on and retain his balance by.

So let us suppose you do find yourself fighting out the finish: keep hold of your horse's head, sit poised over his neck and ride him out with hands and heels in time with the rhythm of his stride, maintaining contact with his mouth, perhaps just slapping him down the shoulder and *willing* the post to come when his head is in front; keep your eyes a stride ahead of the winning post so that you don't inadvertently relinquish your efforts a stride too soon; and *on no account* look round. By doing so, you may not only unbalance your horse and lose concentration yourself, but if you look one away, there may be a rival creeping up the other.

If you have ridden a neat, tidy finish but get beaten half a length in your first race you may think, 'I would have won if I had whacked him,' but the chances are you would have been beaten further or fallen off at the last.

David Tatlow says:

To learn to be calm in a finish is vital, and one of the hardest things; tired horses don't want, need or expect a tired rider bumping up and down all over the place.

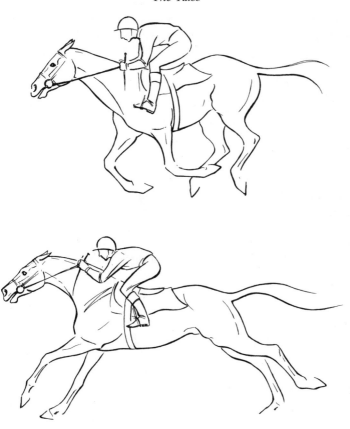

Riding a horse out with hands and heels; the jockey must remain in rhythm with his mount

If you want to find out what it's like, put half a hundredweight of sand on your back, fasten it securely and run around; then put on a quarter of a hundredweight loosely, run around with it flopping about, and see which is the more tiring. It's quite a good exercise and one you will never forget!

Once you have passed the post, don't pull up too hurriedly; this applies equally if you have the misfortune to feel your horse break down in the race: you must still pull up gradually to prevent worsening the damage. The same must be said about pulling up downhill; it causes extra strain on the legs and should be done gently.

Wherever you finish, you are bound to be out of breath, totally hooked and an exhilarated convert to race-riding, full of praise for your horse, and just longing for the next time...

Weighing In

If you finish in the first four you are required to weigh in. Failure to do so will result in the automatic disqualification of your horse. The only exception to this would be if you fell off after the winning post and were injured, or if you became ill after the winning post and were unable to weigh in. Unsaddling enclosures are provided for the first three — sometimes four — horses and here you must unsaddle the horse yourself and proceed straight to the scales, while your helper puts a sweat-sheet on your horse.

It is forbidden to receive any outside assistance in removing your saddle from the horse and carrying it into the scales, unless you have stewards permission to do so; sometimes lightweight girls riding with 12 st. 7 lb. or even 13 st. will need assistance or, for instance, when returning to race riding after sustaining an injury such as a broken collar bone and finding the saddle too heavy to carry. Unless your horse goes lame, you should ride him all the way from the winning post to the unsaddling enclosure which is usually in or right beside the parade ring; make sure you explain what has happened to a steward if unable to do so (if your horse has broken down, for instance). The reason for all this is to prevent any skulduggery: it could be all too easy for an accomplice to slip lead to a dismounted jockey and then he could weigh in as having carried the correct weight when in reality he had cheated.

An accidental occurrence that can happen all too easily is to lose a weight cloth during the race. Here, saddling up is so important, but so is checking the girths at the start. If you lose your cloth in the race and its weight was more than 2 lb., disqualification is automatic. A rider is allowed to lose 2 lb. in a race, as this can be shed in sweat.

At the scales you weigh with everything except your hat and whip and then you are free to see to your horse, to change, to celebrate or commiserate, and to make plans for next time...

Objections and Dope Testing

A brief word here about objecting: don't. It is not a sporting thing to do, and if there has been an occurrence in a race that warrants it, the stewards should have seen it and announce their own enquiry. If they fail to do so, swallow it, and don't go about complaining or being a bad loser in public. Disputes, objections and appeals are covered in section 14 of the *Jockey Club Regulations for Point-to-Point Steeplechases*.

Sometimes the dope-testing vehicle will be in attendance, and if a sample is required from your horse, you must give every assistance. The sample will be sent to the Horseracing Forensic Laboratory at Newmarket for analysis. A list of prohibited substances is contained in note C2 at the back of the Regulations just mentioned.

Falls

It is no use imagining that a keen point-to-point rider, no matter how good either he or his horse is, is going to avoid falls, especially when starting out. Sarah Dawson fell off at the first fence in her first race when her horse stood off outside the wings and literally jumped her off, while Angela Howard-Chappell admitted she 'kept on falling off' to begin with. For both, as with many others, it was a question of learning on the racecourse, and soon they were both doing well.

The essential thing to remember when you have a fall is not to get up until you are sure all the remaining runners have passed by. You can be badly injured through trying to rise just as a horse comes by and giving him no way of avoiding knocking you down again. Instead, curl up in a ball, wrap your arms around your head, and lie still.

Although it can be an almost instinctive reaction for riders experienced in other disciplines, *don't* try to hang on to your horse by the reins as this can pull him round so abruptly that

Coping with a fall:
a) the wrong way to fall; stiff-limbed

b) the correct way to fall; rolling into a ball

c) never rise too quickly

it causes him to break down. If you are able to catch your horse and continue in the race, you have to remount at 'the part of the course where it parted from its rider', this generally being construed as before what would have been the next fence.

Don't try and play the hero by attempting to rise before you are ready to after a fall. Many is the time I have lain on the ground winded but have unfastened tight clothing to assist myself even before first aid has arrived. If you *are* badly injured, there is a fence steward and First Aider, usually of the Red Cross or St John Ambulance Brigade, on hand at every fence, and these volunteers always have efficient means of summoning the doctor and ambulance. It is a Jockey Club requirement that, at every meeting, there should be at least two doctors and two ambulances equipped with airway equipment and scoop stretcher. If you cannot be moved, and the runners are due round again for the second circuit, a marker will be placed in the fence to stop them jumping on to you.

It should be pointed out here that riders still in the race *must* jump the fence, even if the obstruction is in the middle of it, and even if well-meaning onlookers are waving them round. This contentious issue has cropped up on several occasions, but the stewards have never wavered from their policy of disqualification for any fence thus omitted.

It is a rule that after a fall in a point-to-point you are obliged to report to the doctor in the weighing room, and if you are due to ride again that day, he has to pass you fit to do so.

It is also mandatory to belong to the Point-to-Point Riders' Personal Accident Scheme, the premium for this being levied on the rider's certificate. Until 1990 this scheme provided only capital insurance benefits, but nowadays it also provides weekly benefits for temporary total disablement. However, although it is necessary for a race-rider to acknowledge the possibility of falls, there is no purpose in dwelling upon the topic of falls and injuries and, indeed, if a rider ever starts to do so, their time has come to retire.

13

Care of the Horse After and Between Races

At home after a race, treat your horse much as you would after hunting; encourage him to stale and have a roll, then give him a mash or a small feed and his hay. If he has eaten up, give him a bigger feed later on, and if all that has gone by morning, then there is a fair chance you will be able to run him again next week. However, if he fails to clear up his feed or only picks at his hay, or if there is so much as a suspicion of heat in a leg, you will have to wait.

Assuming he has come out of the race sound, well and raring to go again, don't make the mistake of galloping him during the week. He has just had a three mile gallop in the race, and all he wants now is to 'tick over.'

Lead him out the day after the race and let him have a pick of grass; preferably turn him out for an hour or two, to relax and unwind. Ride him out quietly for two days and then midweek let him have a leg stretch, a canter for four or five furlongs, and if you find a different field from previously for a change of scenery, so much the better.

Have a quiet hack out on Thursday, and on Friday give him his pipe-opener, preferably uphill, and probably in the same place as you did before his successful first run, because both you and he will associate it with good things. Finally, if necessary, get the farrier to check his shoes in time to do any work required before the next race.

14

Hunter Chases

It is quite possible that even if you do just moderately well point-to-pointing, you will find your horse has qualified for one of the hunter chase finals. Alternatively you may simply decide to enter a local hunter chase, where third prize money (and sometimes fourth) will probably be more than for winning an open point-to-point.

Although the Land Rover men's opens and RMC Group ladies opens may have good class competitors coming from quite far afield to qualify, qualification nevertheless goes down to third place and, with a choice of many meetings at Easter, or with a lack of runners on firm ground, it may not be too difficult to pick up a third place; and when you discover you have qualified for such a final, it is only natural for the enthusiastic newcomer to want to have a go. *The Times* restricted open series also takes qualifiers down to third place and so, by definition, some of these will be really quite moderate.

The art of race-riding in a hunter chase barely alters from that of a point-to-point although the fences will be a little bit bigger and stiffer, so you must sit that much tighter, be prepared to slip some rein and lean back a bit more in the event of a mistake, and kick that much harder into a fence on a sticky horse. Also, there is always a water jump.

You will feel proud to race on a professional course, but it will have a different atmosphere from that of a local point-to-point, being more formal and with a much wider spectrum of spectators, and fewer faces familiar to you.

Also, there is considerably more 'red tape'. For a point-to-point, only the horse is registered with Weatherby's but, to run under N.H. rules, not only must the colours be registered, but so must the owner; also the jockey must hold an amateur rider's permit. Application forms for these registrations are obtainable from the registry office, Weatherby's, Sanders Road, Wellingborough, Northants.

The entry system is also different, now being based on five-day entry and overnight declaration. Check the race conditions, the time and date of closing of entries and of declaration. Detailed notes on how to do this are contained in the back of the *Jockey Club Regulations for Point-to-Point Steeplechases*.

The list of entries and weights will be available via the Wellingborough computer by 1 p.m. on the day following closure of entries. The entries can be viewed on Prestel, and are available from the Press. An entry may be made by telephone to Weatherby's on 0933−440011; each individual is safeguarded by his or her own security code, a bit like a PIN number with credit cards. Anyone who has held one of these the previous season will be allocated it again automatically but, if hunter chasing for the first time, you will need to apply to the Racing Calendar Office for your own code number.

Security and checking are doubly safeguarded by the fact that all telephone calls concerning entries are tape-recorded. Weatherby's will ask you the race number and name for which you wish to enter (which will have appeared in the 'Races to Close' section of the *Racing Calendar*, and from which you should have checked the conditions of the race to ensure your horse is eligible). The information you give will be entered into the computer by the operator and checked back with you. You will then give the name of the horse you wish to enter and the name of the owner; the operator then gives you a unique entry reference number, so that no malpractor can try and withdraw or declare without your knowledge. The computer will give the horse's age and sex to check qualification on those grounds. If your horse is at livery, you must register an Authority to Act if the livery proprietor is to make entries and generally act on your behalf. Entries may also be made by letter, fax or telex.

When you enter for a hunter chase, you have to declare to

run by 10 a.m. (or 10.30 a.m. if so stated) the *previous* day. Another important thing to remember when declaring for a hunter chase is that if your horse wears blinkers these, too, have to be declared. If you fail to do so, the horse will not be allowed to run in them.

One of the features of the entry system is a Help Desk to assist anyone with problems or queries concerning their entry. Help and assistance for the newcomer are very much part and parcel of the point-to-point scene also, and it is this willingness to embrace the newcomer that epitomises the whole hunt racing scene; an *esprit de corps* that permeates throughout the ranks of an amateur sport which is, after all, truly a great leveller...

Conclusion

Even years after hanging up my boots, if I am watching at the last fence and see a rider approaching it on a tight rein, the horse full of running and jumping superbly, a big lump wells up. It is not the disappointments I remember, but the fifteen years of fun — and I hope this book will encourage others to embark on that same adventure, bringing rewards and memories to last a lifetime.

Bibliography

Horse and Hound, IPC Magazines, published weekly.

Instructions for Point-to-Point Steeplechases, Jockey Club Point-to-Point Liaison Committee, 1992.

Jockey Club Regulations for Point-to-Point Steeplechases, Registry Office of the Jockey Club, 1992.

Point-to-Pointing, Terence Brady and Michael Felton, Pelham Books, 1990.

Steeplechasing, John Hislop, J.A. Allen (second edn), 1982.

Your First Point-to-Point Horse, Joe Hartigan, J.A. Allen, 1975.

A

Useful Addresses

British Equestrian Insurance, Hildenbrook House, The Slade, Tonbridge, Kent.

Frank Dick, Physical Trainer, 38 Ormiston Grove, London, W12 0JT.

Horse and Hound, Kings Reach Tower, Stamford Street, London, SE1 9LS.

Jockey Club, 42 Portman Square, London, W1H 0EN.

Jockey Club Point-to-Point Liaison Committee, joint Secretaries, Simon Claisse, Registry Office of the Jockey Club (as above) and Anthony Hart, Master of Foxhounds Association, Parsloes Cottage, Bagendon, Cirencester, Glos.

Point-to-Point Owners Association, Secretary, Mrs. J. Dawson, 'Crispins', 90A. Ellis Road, Crowthorne, Berkshire, RG11 6PN.

Point-to-Point Secretaries Association, Chair, Mrs. C. Higgon, Newton Hall, Crundale, Haverfordwest, Pembrokeshire.

Weatherby's, Racing Calendar Office, Sanders Road, Wellingborough, Northants, NN8 4BX.

B

Area Schedules

Area schedules may be obtained by sending a 10″ × 7″ stamped, addressed envelope to:

Devon and Cornwall
M Hawkins Esq
Hunters Lodge
Newton St Cyres,
Exeter Devon

Tel: 0392 851275 (home)
      0392 423834 (office)

East Anglia
V Hunter Rowe Esq
Curles Manor
Clavering
Saffron Walden
Essex CB11 4PW

Tel: 0799 550283

Midlands
The Hon Mrs R L Newton
Church Farm
Saltby, Melton Mowbray Leics

Tel: 0476 860240
      0476 860221 (home)

Northern
C Sample Esq
South Middleton, Scots Gap
Morpeth Northumberland

Tel: 0670 74245 (home)
      0670 513128 (office)

North Western
J R Wilson Esq
Huntingdon House
Little Wenlock, Telford Salop

Tel: 0952 502354 (home)
      0425 470133 (office)

South Midlands
Col. A Clerke Brown OBE
Kingston Grove
Kingston Blount, Oxon OX9 4SQ

Tel: 0844 51356

South Wales
P H Curry Esq
South Cottage
Penmark, Barry, S Glamorgan

Tel: 0446 710439 (home)

Taunton
F G Matthews Esq
Peak Ashes
Chapel Lane, Penselwood
Wincanton, Somerset

Tel: 0747 840412

Welsh Border
J R Pike Esq
The Priory
Kilpeck, Hereford

Tel: 0981 21366

Sandhurst
P A D Scouller Esq
Bottom House Bix
Henley on Thames, Oxon RG9 6DF

Tel: 0491 574776 (home)
0734 874311 (office)

West Midlands
Mrs S Newell
Woodhall
Norton, Worcs WR5 2RR

Tel: 0905 351864

Yorkshire
Catherine Wardroper
Low Carr
Ampleforth, York YO6 4ED

Tel: 03476 600 (home)
04393 771 (office)

South East
J C S Hickman Esq
Romney House
Ashford Market
Elwick Road Ashford Kent

Tel: 0233 622222

West Wales
Cynthia Higgon
Newton Hall
Crundale, Haverfordwest Dyfed

Tel: 0437 731239